GW00739319

THE CAT ZODIAC

THE CAT ZODIAC

WITH ILLUSTRATIONS BY SUSAN ROBERTSON
& John Francis

HAMLYN

CONTENTS

FOREWORD by Russell Grant 7

ARIES	9	LIBRA	45
TAURUS	15	SCORPIO	51
GEMINI	21	SAGITTARIUS	57
CANCER	27	CAPRICORN	63
LEO	33	AQUARIUS	69
VIRGO	39	PISCES	75

ACKNOWLEDGEMENTS 80

First published in 1988 by the
Hamlyn Publishing Group Limited,
a division of the Octopus Publishing Group,
Michelin House
81 Fulham Road
London SW3 6RB

© The Hamlyn Publishing Group Limited, 1988

ISBN 0-600-56007-4

Typeset by MS Filmsetting, Frome, Somerset
Colour origination by Mandarin, Hong Kong
Printed by Mandarin Offset in Hong Kong

All rights reserved.
No part of this publication may be reproduced,
stored in a retrieval system, or transmitted,
in any form or by any means, electronic,
mechanical, photocopying, recording or
otherwise, without the permission of the
publisher and the copyrightholder.

FOREWORD

The astrologically uninitiated, sceptical or suspicious, find it difficult to accept that the planets have an influence on human beings, let alone animals. The more enlightened understand that all creatures live under the same cosmic influences but, even so, don't always apply this to their pets. The ego of the owner can crush the identity of an animal, expecting it to follow commands and obey the master's will. The cat, that most independent of domestic animals, is surely the best equipped to resist these human influences and follow its own star. Acceptance, faults and all, is demanded, and made easier if you have an understanding of your cat's behaviour.

I have never ceased to be amazed at the precise ways my own cats have shown the habits of their sun signs. My first cat was a Pisces, black with a soupçon of Siamese. From the moment of her rebirth as Tamarisk (originally named Meg, she had come from our local RSPCA centre), she displayed all the characteristics of her sun sign: slightly dreamy, hypnotic eyes and an amazing walk. She would tune into my psychic vibes when I read the Tarot, appearing as if from nowhere. Many stunned consultors took this as a sign that the spirit was drawing near; they were probably right – the vibrations must have been whirring around to entice Tamarisk in!

About two years after adopting Tamarisk, I purchased Tarragon and Coriander, two long-haired tabby Geminis – and yes, they were twins. Unfortunately, after playing follow-my-leader for several days, both caught 'flu and had to be put down. Like most twins they did everything together, to the end.

My penchant for ginger cats resulted in Bob's appearance on the scene, at which point the negative side of Tamarisk's nature reared its head and spat and snarled her displeasure. The final straw for Tamarisk came when shortly after acquiring Bob I offered refuge to a deserted Burmese. It was hate at first sight – the fur literally flew. After just one night the poor old Burmese hand-me-down had to be handed on before its already fragile mental state (it was probably a Gemini) was completely shot to pieces. Bob proved more resilient and Tamarisk eventually learned to tolerate his presence; she had the final word, though, by living to the venerable age of 17 and thus outlasting him by six years. Bob was as courageous an Arian cat as could be imagined, but also amorous and ardent. Like most Aries males he was a real pushover if he loved you and would come running from far and wide to have his tummy tickled before embarking on yet another hunt. He was a lovely cat to have around.

Finally, to my current feline companions, Tinker and Archie. Tinker is the silliest, cuddliest Cancerian you could meet. He and his sister Flora were discovered in a dustbin near my home. After a gargantuan Piscean nursing job on my part, they survived. I found a good home for Flora and kept Tinker who, when fully recovered, decided never to leave home again. Suggest a romp in the fields to him and he runs a mile (well, 103 yards, actually, under the bed!); and whenever I go away he pines and refuses his food (very Cancerian!). Archie, my punk Leo, couldn't be more different. He's not insecure and doesn't constantly need reassurance – like many human Leos, mess up his handsome mane and he'll grab you by the arm and throw you into a double nelson!

Well, I hope all this has helped you realize that there's more to most cats than meets the eye. For those people who don't feel comfortable about the idea of having a personal astrological chart prepared for their cat, this book provides the next best thing. Who knows, eventually you may even find yourself questioning the belief that it is dog alone who is man's best friend!

Russell Grant

ARIES

21ST MARCH – 20TH APRIL

 OLATILE, ASSERTIVE, ENERGETIC, LUSTY – the Arian cat is a catalogue of extrovert qualities and must be given free rein to explore the world and establish its own territory. The cat which sat on the mat was certainly not born under the sign of Aries.

The Arian cat is an outdoor type, but needs the busy variety of a town or city rather than idyllic rural surroundings. Perhaps the Arian could be happy living on a farm, with plenty of activity and a variety of situations to explore – though once the Arian has cut a swathe through the farmyard the other occupants will never feel quite the same again. But it is the rooftops, back alleys and walled yards and gardens of a thriving town that form the ideal adventure playground for an Aries. The more physical obstacles there are, the better – it's a chance to work off some of that extraordinary energy. The neighbourhood inhabitants, human or feline, simply add to the challenge and stretch this cat's ingenuity: the male Arian will never duck the challenge posed by a resident tomcat, nor miss the opportunity to woo and win a pretty queen.

Despite the differences bestowed by Nature on the lifestyles of male and female cats, you won't notice so much difference in behaviour when it comes to Arian felines. Both toms and queens are independent and adventurous. The Arian tom is a complete Casanova (that highly successful philanderer was also born under the sign of Aries). He will sometimes be out for days and nights on end, fighting off the opposition and establishing his claim to all the most beautiful females for miles around. But disappointment is in store for the queen who hopes to tame the Arian tom by coquettish and wilful behaviour. He will be fascinated for a while, but quickly becomes bored and moves on if his desires are not accomplished – and there is always somewhere, or someone, to move on to where the Arian is concerned.

The female Arian is a born flirt, and though she may return more often to home-base than her male counterpart, she will spend plenty of time out and about, charming her local swains and preening herself in front of her jealous rivals. This cat makes a good mother if the time arrives, but when her duty is done and the kittens are ready to make their way into the world alone, she will be more than happy to resume her independence. And even if she is all too aware of her own attractions, she is an elegant and pleasurable sight when enthroned on a high wall or basking on a sunny balcony.

Arian energy does not take time to build up steam – it is inborn and only awaiting release. From the moment its eyes open, the Arian kitten sees that the world is full of lots of places to go and things to play with. It is an exhausting prospect for its feline mother or for its long-suffering surrogate family of humans. Nothing is safe from Arian investigation – which is always of a highly physical nature. This kitten will tunnel under the lifted corner of a rug, tweak pretty flowers out of vases, and pull on every dangling thread it ever sees. This may be charming in a tiny kitten, but beware the signs as it becomes a young and sturdy cat: that persistent interest in the corner of a tablecloth is sooner or later going to bring the entire contents of the tea-table down on your playful friend's head. Except that, with the cat's quick instinct for impending disaster, it will already be far away, leaving someone else to deal with the aftermath of its action.

The Arian kitten is also a terrific clown, and whenever in sight will provide a continual display of acrobatic feats – climbing, jumping, juggling – that could keep a crowd amused for hours. With adulthood, all this activity becomes more graceful and purposeful.

Since Arians spend little time at home, their human friends have few opportunities to get to know them better. In fact, there is little more to know – Aries has a splendidly straightforward character, and what you see is what you get. This simplicity is refreshing, but can cause occasional problems. Sensitivity is not one of the strongest points with this sign, and your cat may not notice that you would from time to time like to be acknowledged during its rare perambulations through the house. Aries is also the possessor of an impulsive nature and a fiery temper, which dies down as quickly as it flares. Being physically expressive, the Arian cat enjoys being stroked and cuddled and loves to be the centre of attention, but at a certain point it will become bored with the game and think of something better to do. An unexpected hiss or scratch may be the first you know of its change of mind; though maliciousness is not in the cat's character, it will provide definite signals when it wishes to be left alone.

There are certain qualities you need if you are going to share your life successfully with an Aries – particularly an Arian tom, to whom there are no holds barred. You must be equipped with an even disposition, not to be disrupted by the now-you-see-me-now-you-don't playfulness of this feline character, and a complete absence of anxiety, to last out the long periods when your furry friend stays away from home; you require, in other words, a deep sense of personal security, because the Arian will test your equanimity to the limit. But if you feel up to the challenge, the Arian's strong character and busy lifestyle can provide the greatest interest and enjoyment.

An invitation to disaster in Zodiac pairings is issued when a Virgo takes on an Arian cat. This sign is too obsessed with order and cleanliness to appreciate the havoc that an active Arian can cause. Those born under Cancer should also be wary of seeking companionship with Aries. A Cancerian is too fond of home to appreciate a live-in friend who treats the place as a hotel, just stopping for a quick wash and brush up before going out on the tiles again.

An Arian person could be the perfect match for the feline Aries, each too busy with their own concerns to worry about the other, but physically and mentally well suited on the occasions when they do get together. The only danger here is that two such self-interested parties could run into a clash of wills over relatively minor issues. A similar pairing is Leo and Aries, two signs which both carry great vigour and charm, but again with the slight risk that a competitive element could get out of hand.

An excellent partnership, especially from the Arian point of view, is that between Aries and Libra. The selflessness of Libra supports the Arian's more demanding nature, and Aries supplies the energy which Librans need to overcome their languid moments. Gemini and Sagittarius are both signs which are sufficiently active and quick-witted to cope with the busy physicality of Aries, and the cerebral but unconventional Aquarian can also appreciate the Arian's vitality and complete lack of deviousness.

SMALL-SCREEN STAR

Herb was an alleycat, a smart-guy survivor. He had gained his name from the local bag-ladies because he usually smelled a bit sweeter than the other cats, which wasn't saying much for him. Abandoned early on by a wayward mother, Herb learned to survive by scavenging on the streets. This clever cat had acquired a trick that put him ahead of his rivals in the food-snatch business and left him a little sleeker than the rest. When some good scraps were spotted among a pile of garbage, it was a case of first come first served. Herb's neat tactic was to dart a paw into a crumpled can or battered paper sack, hook out the tastiest part of the contents and flick it into the air, catching it in his mouth as it flew over the scrawny shoulders of the other cats. They, naturally, sometimes resent-ed his better fortune, but few could figure out exactly how the trick worked, and none was fast enough to beat Herb to the prize.

This state of affairs lasted a year or so, and Herb had made it into adulthood a handsome if occa-sionally dishevelled specimen. Only one battle scar was visible – the cloven tip of one ear, torn by a tigerish opponent. Little did Herb know that this was part of the credentials that qualified him for a style of life he could never have imagined.

Herb had the luck, all the other cats knew it, and Herb's luck was surely working on the day he was spotted by an advertising man who was waiting for a bus. The ad-man was not accus-tomed to wait for buses too often, but it had been a bad day. As it happened, the bus stop stood opposite the entrance to an alley where Herb and his friends often found particularly good pickings. And so it was that the ad-man witnessed Herb performing his trick. He watched in mounting admiration as the rangy cat flipped food into his mouth with effortless style.

It wasn't easy to catch Herb, but the ad-man was filled with excitement and determination. How easy was it to get a new angle for a catfood account? Everything had been tried. In Herb a star was born; fame and fortune were in the can. After a night of furtive activity, the next morning a puzzled Herb was parked in a well-appointed cat basket on the ad-agency's deep-pile carpet.

Problem was, faced with an open can full of food, Herb just put his head down and hoovered up the contents. It took a while for the ad-man to get Herb to perform, street-style, his special flip and catch. Seeing that his colleagues were getting bored and disbelieving, the ad-man crossly snatched the food away from Herb – who, sure enough, whipped out a paw towards the receding can and, scooping out a pawful of food, flicked it into his mouth. Applause, applause.

During a short but intense period of training, Herb finally grasped the fact that the food-flip trick was his passport to success. Meantime, he was gradually growing heavy and glossy. The raggedy ear, after fierce debate among people whose business was packaging and presenting images, was claimed as a charming symbol of Herb's leaner days, a device intended to enhance his aura as a popular hero.

Came the day for the cameras to roll and the rest, as they say, is history. Herb was appearing twice-nightly on television screens across the country;

he was soon in demand for opening hypermarkets and appearing at galas. He acquired a spacious home (property deeds in his own name, had he known or cared), ate hugely and travelled in style. Herb became famous as a go-getter, the role model for aspiring members of his species.

And was there a secret cost to all this fame and fortune? Did he lie awake nights in the lonely agonies of the suddenly successful? Not Herb: he took it all in his stride. Just Herb's luck was all it was, ask any alleycat.

TAURUS

21ST APRIL – 21ST MAY

TAUREANS LIVE UP TO THE IMAGE OF THEIR ZODIAC SYMBOL BY being both bull-necked and, at times, bull-headed, but there is no companion more faithful or generous than a secure and satisfied Taurus. This happy condition is brought about by offering the Taurean cat a comfortable home, supportive friendship – and an endless supply of excellent food. This animal does not nurture eccentric tastes or extraordinary ambitions: it wants good, solid home comforts from cradle to grave, and matches this by growing into a good, solid house cat mainly modest in its requirements.

The way to the Taurean heart is definitely through the stomach. Heavy build is characteristic of Taureans, so this cat has a large frame to fill with suitable nourishment and can do a convincing imitation of a vacuum cleaner whenever an appetizing plate of meat is within range. The hearty appetite should be carefully monitored,

however, because obesity is never far away from a fully grown Bull-cat. It can develop into the kind of giant cat which gets its picture in the local newspaper and becomes a neighbourhood celebrity for doing nothing more remarkable than ambling around the garden or gazing at the world from the safety of a (broad) windowsill.

Such weightiness is likely to be a concomitant of laziness. While Taureans are not naturally the most active of cats neither are they necessarily idle, but an overweight specimen will move from its chair only to consume yet another meal. That chair, incidentally, is the large fireside chair, covered with a luxurious fabric and fitted with comfortable cushions, that you saved for since starting to furnish your first home. Once the Taurean has spotted this item as a desirable residence, it will take possession at every opportunity. If you settle down by the fire for the evening, forget about getting up to make a cup of coffee: by the time you come back, the cat will be firmly installed in your chair. It really is best to give in gracefully and obtain two similar seats where you and the cat can adopt a Darby and Joan routine undisturbed by one another – but be sure to let the Taurean choose its place first, or the bloodless battle will begin again.

This situation relates to another particularly Taurean trait – an active enjoyment of individual possessions. While any cat can operate the well-known feline talents for falling asleep on its feet or eating off the draining board, Taureans much prefer to have their own chair, bed and crockery distinctly identified and reserved for personal use. When you move house with a Taurean cat in tow, it will spend the first few days inspecting the new arrangements and overseeing your attempts to unpack and make the place straight. All must be

approved before life can resume the normal patterns which Taureans so much desire – and the cat will make sure that you manoeuvre its prized objects into the best possible location before settling to the domestic round once again.

As Taurus is the sign associated with the voice, you may be sure the Taurean cat will speak out loud and clear in any situation which is not to its liking. This is sometimes an attractive prospect, as the Taurean probably has a throaty bass or contralto miaow, rather than the shrill complaining range beloved of less stable members of the species. When all is well, the Taurean purr can enter a decibel level which could qualify as noise-pollution, were it not for the fortunate fact that the rhythmic interior tone of purring is invariably a delightful sound.

Being very much attached to its home, the Taurean spends a lot of time indoors and generally exceeds the feline average of two-thirds of its life spent asleep. This is an unusually relaxed and easy-going character who certainly has no difficulty unwinding. Being equable types, Taureans are well suited to being put in charge of a multi-cat household: the Taurean sits as solid as a rock amid

the games and squabbles of younger or more volatile colleagues, and will flatten them with a giant paw when things get out of hand. Taurus is slow to anger, but on those rare occasions when the Taurean is provoked beyond endurance, any errant kitten will be in no doubt that it is witnessing the wrath of God.

The Taurean cat ambles outdoors from time to time to indulge a favourite hobby – a little light gardening. As your flowerbeds become pitted with small quarries and molehills, you can trace the cat's passage. There is no special routine to the activity, nor any specific purpose; it is just a vaguely relaxing form of exercise far more amenable to the character of Taurus than anything deliberately athletic.

Territorial domination is not a problem to the male Taurean – what is out of sight is out of mind. Should a challenger approach within the domestic range of the Taurean tom, it may be in for a nasty surprise. The dozing beast, which to the intruder's eye appeared stupidly uncomprehending of its danger, finds it less trouble to fight than to flee when finally aroused, so the Taurean rises slowly to his feet and allows his massive bulk to inflate before his rival's terrified gaze. If this is not sufficient deterrent, the mighty bull-necked head goes down and the Taurean takes aim. A feline Bull in full charge is an unstoppable force, and few other cats are prepared to play the role of an immovable object; nor are they likely to have a scientific curiosity about what might happen after the point of impact.

A Taurean cat is never a troublesome house-mate, unless you are likely to be disturbed by stability, but there is an occasional tendency towards complete inertia in Taureans which makes them less than ideal companions for impatient Arians or mischievous Aquarians. A Gemini may be too independent and active to appreciate the fixedness of Taurus, and Sagittarians in search of new experiences may find themselves exasperated by the Taurean preference to remain a creature of habit immune to exploratory influences.

There are good qualities in a match between Virgo and Taurus, as the Virgoan pride in good housekeeping caters well to the Taurean appreciation of well-kept surroundings, but problems can arise from the fact that Virgo is a mutable sign and Taurus the most fixed. Leo and Taurus are such strong personalities that a bond between them is unassailable by external forces, but should a difference of opinion arise at home there will be no compromise and no solution.

Cancer, Capricorn, Libra and Pisces are peaceable people who appreciate the relaxed presence of a Taurean: Cancerians and Taureans particularly are both tactile types who will develop a close physical bond, literally staying in touch with each other. Scorpio has almost opposite preoccupations to those of Taurus, but this can create an excellent partnership provided the Scorpio character is not too easily bored. Perhaps the perfect human partner for a feline Taurean is another Taurus: both will consider it of primary importance to establish a comfortable and stable home which can be enjoyed at life-long leisure.

NOAH'S CHOICE

When Noah was commanded to take his animals into the ark, he must have been under no illusion that there were difficult decisions ahead, not the least his initial selection of suitable candidates to be the sole surviving representatives of their species. With limited time to prepare, he needed to depend upon seeing the obvious virtues of individual animals.

The choice of a cat to become the new father of its species fell, as it happened, upon a Taurean male. The attributes of a stout heart and mind contained within an equally sturdy body seemed the equipment of a natural survivor. It was noticed that the cat had an equable temperament occasionally moved to righteous wrath, but nevertheless it bore no grudges and never behaved wilfully or maliciously. The apparent lack of sensitivity sometimes observed in its behaviour was counted as a favourable point; it was unlikely to become depressed by a rather claustrophobic atmosphere, or by the continual beating of a rainstorm scheduled to last for forty tedious days and nights. Whereas an arrogant Leo might upset its companions, or a fatherly Cancerian might become over-anxious on their behalf, the Taurean cat could be counted upon to plod through the ordeal as peaceably as possible, its rock-like presence a calming influence upon the more nervous animal inhabitants of the crowded ark.

The major disadvantage in the Taurean character is its bullish resistance to radical change; and here was coming the greatest change since the creation of the world. Yet the Taurean was also a pragmatic type and, once installed in the ark, peering out at the continual rain, would surely come to the conclusion that since it was unable to return the status quo to the previous, certainly preferable conditions, it might as well deal with the present to the best of its abilities.

In due course, as the animals went into the ark two by two, the Taurean cat boarded unhurriedly with its chosen mate; who else but a female Taurean, a real earth mother with a solid temperament perfectly matched to that of her consort? Because cats are an agile and easily portable package, it was of course not necessary to confine them as the greater beasts such as lions and elephants had to be shut away, so they were able to roam freely about the interior of the ark, becoming familiar with all the animal and human occupants. They were under strict orders not to take advantage of the birds and tiny creatures which shared the closeted spaces within the ship; but all the animals instinctively understood the extremity of their situation, and a kind of truce reigned throughout the months of close company.

The account of the ark's voyage provides little detail of arrangements for feeding this floating zoo. Certainly Taureans do not function at their most efficient if deprived of fuel, so it may be assumed that supplies were adequate to enable the animals to survive in reasonable comfort. The Taurean cats retained a secret weapon against the more distasteful or depressing aspects of the adventure – their ability to fall asleep in a split second and catnap soundly amid the chaotic noise which would necessarily arise from such a conglomeration of beasts.

When finally the flood began to subside, the cats stood on either side of Noah each time the dove was sent out from the ark to investigate the condition of the earth. Wisely they understood the significance of the olive leaf returned on the dove's penultimate mission. Gladly they welcomed the beautiful rainbow which stretched across the receding clouds, a sign as they set foot on dry land that the stability of the earth's surface was reintroduced and would henceforth be protected.

GEMINI

22ND MAY – 21ST JUNE

HOW MANY CATS MAKE FIVE? If they are Geminis, the answer is an infinite number. In the sign of the Twins you might expect duality, but Geminis do not stop there; each is an entire cast of characters, constructed out of the exuberant energy and wide-ranging interests typical of the Geminian. The Gemini cat is the perfect companion for the young at heart and itself retains a kittenish curiosity about the world that keeps it in lively spirits most of the time. There is such a thing as a depressed Geminian, but as this is a boring condition a true Gemini cannot suffer it for long and will soon perk up and find something much more worthy of investigation than the inside of its own head.

Geminians are communicative types and language is a continual delight, so be prepared to pay attention to a cat that vocalizes frequently and variously and takes a particular pleasure in articulating its feelings. It is likely to have a much more distinct vocabulary than may be discerned in other cats, having dozens of ways to ask for milk or food and a quite different range of sounds to signify wishing to be let out, including such nuances as 'Check first if it's raining' and 'Did you fix the hinge on the catflap or am I going to trap my tail again?' Fortunately this is a good-humoured animal who won't hold it against you if its subtler expressions are not fully understood.

A quick brain is a Geminian feature and this is used as a highly efficient databank. Every detail of the cat's surroundings is filed away for present use and possible future emergency. It knows sources of food and water for miles around, the best places for mousing, the locations of interesting bird tables, the sweetest-smelling flowers and the most suitable flowerbeds for toilet use. Not only does it have a mental list of all the hiding places and comfortable cloisters of its own home, it has probably checked out neighbouring houses for alternative haunts. This research project has a doubly appealing purpose, as a secret invasion into next-door territory caters for the Geminian love of risky ventures – other cats, dogs, or non-cat-loving humans unexpectedly encountered during these trips represent an exciting challenge on which the Geminian can sharpen its wits, and possibly its claws as well.

A Gemini is quick-witted enough to get out while the going is good, but if cornered is not going to back away. It will, if necessary, enter upon a good, clean fight and at the end of the proceedings wander off with no hard feelings. A more typically Geminian strategy is, however, to charm the opposition into forgetting about a confrontation. Geminis are naturally gregarious and have a busy social life. A Geminian street cat soon gets on terms with the neighbourhood felines and will cultivate more than a nodding acquaintance with the butcher, the baker and other sources of friendly gifts.

Geminis are lively types and are always fully occupied, but they also need plenty of sleep. As an Air sign, Gemini likes to be surrounded by a fresh, open atmosphere; a roof garden is a wonderful place for the Geminian cat to take private time, which it does need, but it will also soon want to be

back in the hustle and bustle at ground level, where it will appreciate broad walkways, expansive lawns and dappled, tree-lined streets rather than enclosed yards and alleys. A city cat which must live with more crowded circumstances will sure-footedly establish a passage along the highest walls and rooftops to gain access to the airy quality of atmosphere that it loves.

Indoors the Geminian free spirit fares less well; cats of this sign do not relax so easily as some of their peers and can quickly become bored and nervous in an unchanging environment. The Gemini is not the cuddliest of cats, as it is wary of being trapped by over-zealous humans desperate to show their affection; it will be a charming presence, equally gracious towards strangers or

friends, but in all types of relationships it prefers to participate on its own terms. Nevertheless, this cat does not lack affection for its daily companions and it will happily show this in ways that do not risk total engagement: the cat's typical hop-up greeting, simultaneously rubbing its head against a person's legs, is the perfect expression of love from the lively Gemini. Otherwise it may sit close by you, uttering the strange cheeps and chirrups that communicate its appreciation of intelligent companionship. It is not well-equipped for quiet contemplation, however, and if not lulled to sleep by the comfortable closeness will soon interest itself in anything that moves within its range.

Movement is a particular pleasure to Geminians and their own graceful demonstrations are not the only means of enjoyment. Pushing papers off the table, pulling cushions out of chairs, twisting flowers out of vases, fishing forks out of the washing-up bowl: anything which is free-standing and not too physically heavy for the cat to move will sooner or later come unhitched from its rightful place. Geminis are, it must be said, untidy types who can unwittingly wreak havoc on a home with their constant activity. Life is a great adventure for Geminis, even in the smallest details, and these are cats to be lived alongside, not kept in their own place like selected possessions.

Imagine a pairing of Geminis, one human, one feline; together they make a constant chattering, bridging the communication gap in their own inimitable ways, while neither is offended nor inclined to feel neglected when the other is busy elsewhere. Virgo, too, is a communicative sign and like Gemini not physically possessive, so this is an excellent partnership. Aquarius has similar qualities endearing to the Gemini soul. Aries and Gemini are able to make a good match, both active personalities capable of inspiring each other with mutual enthusiasm. The same can be said of Leos and Geminians, with the caution that Gemini's mutability can stretch the tolerance of the basically stable Leo.

Problems can arise in any attempt to establish relations between Pisces and Gemini; the Piscean is a caring and occasionally anxious type who may be disturbed by Gemini's footloose and fancy-free attitude to life. The same is true for Cancer, the natural parent, who may be made moody and insecure by the comings and goings of a furry Geminian friend. That element of restlessness is also unappealing to Scorpio people, who may assume that the Geminian is superficial and not take time to investigate its finer points. Taurus makes a firm anchorage for Gemini's outgoing character, but generally likes to be more in touch physically than mentally and may make the Geminian feel trapped.

Librans share sociability, grace and charm with Geminians and this can be a harmonious, elegant association. Both are Air signs and therefore complementary, but it is the Fire sign Sagittarius which can get the best out of Gemini. These are opposite signs in the Zodiac circle, which is always auspicious, and Sagittarians are among the few who can outdo Gemini in both mental agility and physical adventurousness.

Joe, The Trucker

A life on the open road is the way in which a clever Geminian cat called Joe has chosen to satisfy his taste for adventure and variety. He hasn't had to sacrifice a certain sense of security, however. Joe has hitched himself to a trucker, a friendly tough guy whose business is transcontinental freight, and who is pleased enough to have an intelligent, easy-going companion on his long-haul trips. These two buddies, Joe and Frank, ride the road together for days at a time. In between assignments they return to a small house in a small country town outside a big city. Here they have many friends and acquaintances, but few ties. Neither thinks he has lost out on anything by his vagabond existence. Both have a certain restlessness and a need to feel space around themselves, so they are both of the opinion that their lifestyle suits them pretty well.

When they're working, these two sleep in the truck of a night; it has been fitted out nicely with everything they need. In the back of the high driver's cab is a platform which holds a narrow mattress and some bedding. In the storage section of the cab, Frank keeps a camper's stove, which he uses to make a brew when the fancy takes him, a cooler to hold any fresh stuff that they pick up on their way, and a supply of cans of Joe's preferred catfood, together with a very reliable can opener. At some of their stops along the way Joe is quite a favourite with the staff of the roadside cafes. When there are not too many people around, he can go in with his buddy and pick a burger to pieces while Frank works his way through a giant plateful. (Joe is pretty partial to tomato relish but he doesn't care for fries.) These two are an attractive pair, and have more than once been asked to stay on and act sociable. But they always have an instinct for when it's time to leave, and no enticement has seriously tempted them to discard their footloose ways.

Out on the highway, Joe sits up front of the cab and misses nothing that passes. He chatters at grazing cows seen in distant fields and flocks of birds passing low over grain-growing land. When he and Frank are both feeling talkative, they each get going on a monologue and their ideas pleasantly intertwine in Frank's low drawl and Joe's busy chirrups and miaows. Sometimes Frank sings to pass the time and Joe occasionally, if rather tunelessly, joins him. Joe knows better than to distract Frank while he's concentrating on some tricky driving, and they both enjoy the periods of companionable silence when there's nothing to say but all is well. When they get to a destination, Joe waits in the cab while the truck is unloaded, unless it's a stop he knows well, when he gets out and strolls off to greet some acquaintances. Their schedules are usually easily met, but sometimes they like to drive on into the night just for the hell of it.

Being on the open road in the truck, Frank and Joe reckon, is the finest feeling known to man or cat. They enjoy the vista of raw-coloured fields stretching on either side of a fast freeway, the dappled shade of tall trees lining the roadside, the flashes of other lives being played out around them as they breeze through the outskirts of a

large town. They love the sun, but take a special excitement from driving through lashing rain, safe inside the cab while the heavy wipers scrape the screen and the low sky threatens. All these things give them a surer sense of belonging to the world than they could find in a more routine or settled existence.

You might get a glimpse of them one day, driving into a spectacular sunset together, and if you can catch the expressions on their faces, you'll know you have seen two of life's most satisfied customers.

CANCER

THE CANCERIAN CAT IS GOING TO ACQUIRE ITSELF A FAMILY, LIKE IT OR NOT, so once you have installed a Cancerian in your home, prepare to play host to a cat refuge. The imperative for Cancer is to go forth and multiply – except that these home-loving creatures prefer to stay in, and still multiply. The ideal solution is to take on a pair of Cancerians and let them raise litter after litter, none of whom will ever be allowed to leave home. In those houses where there is a cat on every cushion and at least one on each bookshelf, cats in bed, in the bathroom and strategically positioned at sentry posts all the way up the stairs, undoubtedly somewhere in the picture there is a Cancerian cat making its rounds in a matronly fashion, ensuring that everyone is fed, washed and happy and that none of the brood has strayed too far for too long.

The famous independence of cats is practically cancelled when the cat in question is born under Cancer. A solitary Cancerian cat is a miserable animal indeed. Do not be misled into thinking you can beat the mothering instinct by having the cat neutered. The Cancerian goes in for surrogate parenting and if it cannot entice in the neighbourhood cats and assemble them into the next best thing to a family unit, you may come home one day to find a curious assortment of rabbits, guinea pigs, and even the odd good-natured dog. Any animal living nearby is a candidate for furnishing your Cancerian cat's capacious nest.

If you persist in trying to convert a Cancerian to single cathood, its alternative strategy is to seek a more sympathetic ambience. To this end it may hang about on the sidewalk beaming at strangers until it finds a likely soft touch, when it will get itself taken home and within days be installed as a permanent feature, preferably at the head of a collection of other 'stray' cats. Cancerians hate to abandon their roots, however, and this type of behaviour is a real sign of desperation. You can take it that you have hopelessly neglected the cat's needs if you find it graciously hosting a neighbour's dinner party only a few days after it has disappeared from your own front room. The Cancerian cat needs the presence of others at all times, and continual affirmations that it is loved and that its efforts are appreciated. It is not the cat for single-minded career persons or weekend vacationers. Any sign of rejection, even if it is incidental rather than deliberate, is devastating to the Cancerian. Like the Crab symbolizing its birth sign, a rejected Cancerian will go into its shell and can become permanently soured, utterly unable to fulfil its potential.

From this you will have correctly divined that staying out all night is not on the Cancerian cat's agenda. Provided that it is surrounded by a growing family, however, its need to know what is happening in the immediate vicinity is easily satisfied by other members of the brood returning to report their adventures while the Cancer matriarch tenderly washes the mud off their paws and sees to a little light snack, more often than not saved from her own bowl of food. Motherly behaviour is not confined to female Cancerians; the Cancer patriarch is a soft-centred soul who has no objections to role reversal or shared responsibilities in parenting.

With their human family, Cancerians are equally demonstrative and expressions of physical affection are a constant part of the cat's daily round. Every time you sit down, the cat sits with you, like a permanent furry appendage. Cancerians usually have a physical softness matched to their comfortable natures, and this pleasantly padded, curvaceous cat is the perfect companion for an evening of quiet relaxation. It will appreciate, also, lots of soft chairs and cushions. Cancerians are traditionalists in most matters and require a homely atmosphere; the modernism which dictates bare floors and streamlined furnishings is unappealing to such cats.

Emotions rule the hearts and heads of Cancerians and, while they can convert a coal-scuttle into a home, they are not equipped to survive emotional deprivation. They can be moody, although their irritability is often an attempt at armouring themselves against disappointment. At worst, when there are serious troubles on the domestic front, guilt and recrimination set in and can develop into a positive persecution mania. Watch out for signs of incipient paranoia and occasionally mad behaviour, which the cat obviously imagines to be a perfectly sane response. One such sign is a demented crab-like walk, where the cat skippers sideways, unable to figure out where it is going or why: this could mean its grasp on reality is weakening. It should not be necessary to call in the cat psychiatrist, however, as it is always possible to interpret what a Cancerian really needs – emotional support and physical contact, both expressed as directly as possible. Talk to the cat constantly, pick it up, share your business with it. The cat will particularly enjoy accompanying you as you cook and clean – this allows it to reassert its practical nature, and when the house is set to rights and a delicious dinner is on the table and in the cat plate, harmony will reign again.

With regard to eating habits, one other aspect of the Cancerian should be reviewed. The high emotional state in which it lives and its sensitivity to unpleasant atmospheres is often translated physically into severe bouts of indigestion, sometimes aggravated by the Cancerian's tendency to acquire bad eating habits – too much too quickly, or too little too late, due to its busy attention to caring for the needs of others. Feed the Cancerian cat regularly, moderately and with wholesome food to combat this uncomfortable condition, which can cause disgruntled moods. The sign of Cancer rules the stomach; make sure the stomach does not rule the cat.

For those who have fled their original nests long since but occasionally have problems standing up to the big wide world, the Cancerian cat can be a tremendously heartwarming presence to come home to. It is the very essence of domesticity; to shut the door on the day's troubles and settle by the fire with a cuddly Cancerian emitting great rolling purrs is many cat-lovers' idea of heaven. Unfortunately, on occasions motherly love can be experienced as a smothering control, so airy Aquarians and Geminis are the signs most likely to become uncomfortable in the presence of the caring Cancerian; while in turn, the Cancerian cat will be puzzled and hurt if either of these two, or a boisterous Arian, expresses impatience with being loved almost to death. Virgos, also, are a little too cool to submit easily to the crab-like clutch of an emotional Cancerian.

Provided the Cancerian's vulnerable emotions do not get the better of the cat, it will prove a solid comfort to signs which have a touch of the childlike in them, as Leo and Libra in their different ways both do. Homeloving signs such as Taurus and Capricorn can appreciate being fussed over by a Cancerian, even if they may sometimes wish that the roles were reversed. If, on the other hand, this Cancerian cat is an insecure type which has learned to guard its sensitivities, it will appreciate the reliable protection of a Capricorn or Taurus, solid citizens both.

THE OTHER MATRIARCH

Queen Victoria's reported fondness for cats is perhaps surprising in one so frequently remembered as being 'not amused'. Her capacity for amusement would have been tried by a feckless Arian or an arrogant Leo, but who more suited to the Victorian ideal than a Cancerian queen, a pretty, matronly cat, not the least daunted by the prospect of a huge family extending into many generations and a personal estate stretching from the banqueting hall to the stables? No domestic detail would have escaped the feline matriarch of the Victorian household, though, like the Queen-Empress whom she would have wished to emulate, it would not be necessary to visit in person every reach of her far dominions to gain a perfect sympathy with the needs and aspirations of her subjects. What better use for the ever-expanding ranks of her children, grand-children and great-grandchildren than to send them out upon the world to form judicious alliances, spread their well-bred influence, and report frequently and fondly to the mother of them all on any matter of which she might need or desire to have knowledge?

From time to time, however, it seemed appro-priate to mount a royal progress to remind all feline inhabitants of the domain that a stern but caring eye was always upon them. The mysteri-ous presence of the matriarch had to be revealed in actuality at least once to each new generation within the dynasty. After due preparation, there-fore, the queenly Cancerian cat would rise from her accustomed place and begin a stately pro-cession through the palace halls, flanked by a retinue of her finest and most influential sons and daughters. At each stopping point she would pause to commune graciously with her kin, and a gaggle of wide-eyed kittens would be marshalled into line for presentation. Occasionally, some astonished ball of fluff would be so overwhelmed by the event as to behave indecorously. Other kittens would crouch and hold their breath in horror, waiting for the wrath to fall. But the soul of a true mother could not help but override the demands of protocol even under such circum-stances, and the reprobate kitten would remem-ber all its life the kindness with which its untimely reaction was forgiven and forgotten.

Victorian society was known for firmly estab-lished hierarchies which were strictly adhered to at each social level. A cat, however greatly reverenced among its own kind, ranked below dogs indoors and horses outdoors. A summons for admission to the royal apartments was therefore more often given to favoured dogs than to cats. Fortunately the cat population, while obeying the social structure in its outward forms, inwardly harboured the view that this was further indisputable evidence of the stupid dependence of dogs on their human providers.

The feline community proceeded to establish itself very comfortably in the unassigned rooms between the servants' quarters and the apartments of state, where they not only had a wealth of amenities for their own enjoyment, but also could observe the traffic of the household undisturbed, from scurrying servants to visiting dignitaries. In this way much valuable knowledge of the domestic politics of the region was ascertained.

The Victorian sentimentality over animals seemed boundless; it was not only in the best-kept households that the domestic animals might fare much better than some of the lower-order human occupants. Able to keep a respectful and respected distance from external intrigues, the Cancerian queen reigned happily and lived, like the Queen-Empress, to a venerable old age. The burgeoning family was beautifully recorded by specially appointed portrait painters. What a vast canvas was needed for the final group portrait of the Cancerian matriarch's Jubilee year, showing her serene at the centre of a dozen generations of her dynasty; the painting was greatly applauded as a monument to family life and to the benign power of a kindly administered empire.

LEO

24TH JULY – 23RD AUGUST

ORN UNDER THE SIGN OF ITS KINGLY RELATIVE, THE LEO cat loses no time in establishing its rightful place as heir apparent. No Leo goes without, takes second place or practises its talents unseen. This is one cat that does not need patient lessons on using the catflap – it can't wait to get out and make its mark upon the world.

These regal tendencies mean that Leos can be flamboyant and energetic without losing their dignified sense of style. They must be the centre of attention, and you must pay court – along with every other occupant of the surrounding terrain. Look for the highest spot in the landscape and undoubtedly there is the Leo posing on top of it, watching the lower orders going about their business and making sure no invasion threatens. Open aggression is not, however, a favourite exercise for Leos. Becoming king of the castle need not involve actual combat, or at worst, only the necessary minimum. Unfortunately, when the Leo is challenged its occasional talent for empty posturing is rudely exposed and the Cowardly Lion which lives under the skin of the noble beast is soon all too apparent.

The cleverest Leo male can dominate simply through knowing he was born to rule, and uses his impressive physique and devastating gaze to baffle and bow down the opposition whenever possible. The leonine lady is living justification for the female cat's entitlement to be called a queen; her gracious elegance is clearly a cut above the rest. Both sexes present a vivid appearance; the truest Leos glow with the colours of the sun – brilliant shades of yellow, orange and red – but even a black or white Leo can be seen to have the glossiest fur for miles around, and knowing this keeps it scrupulously clean and well-groomed.

Leos make excellent parents – he the proud, indulgent father, she an undomineering but protective mother – and both are loyal mates, although it must be remembered that monogamy is not a specially well-developed feline trait. Like lions living free in their native countries, Leo cats can parallel the behaviour of their giant counterparts, the male establishing his right to recline in royal inactivity once the hierarchy is in place, the female having an innate understanding of how to cater to the needs of the pack without surrendering her obvious singularity.

The average home, however, even when equipped with an extensive garden, bears little relation to the central African plains, and the domestic Leo has obviously acquired behaviour patterns and interests suited to its situation. Leos relax through activity and soon set about making the most of available assets. The athletic Leo readily identifies a well-furnished living room as an excellently equipped gymnasium. Especially on wet days when the great outdoors is unenticing, the Leo is regularly to be seen scaling the curtains or leaping along an obstacle course composed of valuable pieces of furniture and ornaments. And even a sedentary Leo, of which there are relatively few, is willing to engage in some acrobatics to acquire a pedestal where he or she will be shown off to advantage. Whether this is the cabinet for your best china or a hand-carved table usually reserved for a prize potted palm is relevant only as to the sympathetic backdrop it offers for putting the Leo on exhibition. Nothing overrides the Leonian right to be seen and admired, preferably in a spectacular setting.

Leos are natural entertainers, but are not above accepting a little discreet education in how to be a star. Most cats find no interest whatsoever in the flickering, illuminated box which can be such a focal point of human activity; they see no intrinsic value in this curious kaleidoscope. Not so the Leo, who in any case regards the television as an essential platform simply because so many people spend so much time looking at it. When some high-quality entertainment is on offer, the cat sits squarely in front of the screen, or peers over the edge from its higher vantage point, in order to study the elements of a star performance.

As this is the sign that rules the heart, there is a special warmth in the affection of a Leo, often expressed through physical contact. Leos like to play, to be stroked, to snuggle on the sofa; to be reserved is not in their nature. They also like to bring gifts, and will certainly expect you to show great delight in a foraged fish-head or recently deceased mouse when it is deposited at your feet. Be sure to provide applause, attention and flattery. Leos hate to be alone or neglected even momentarily, but they know that friendship is not a one-way transaction and a Leonian can be a loyal, generous and supportive companion.

There is, however, an occasional glimpse of a crafty side to this open-hearted character, and you may more than once have a suspicion that it is cupboard love that is on offer: not that the Leo necessarily makes this distinction – a love of food and love of the provider are simply part of the same package. It is also useful to note that Leos do not take criticism well, so the best way to house-train a tiny Leonian is to praise the positive aspects of its behaviour rather than dwell on its unfortunate lapses.

At their best, Leos are likely to be everybody's friend, the combination of physical attractiveness, energy and generosity being almost irresistible. Aries and Leo is an excellent pairing of two very active and dynamic signs. Geminis, too, have a liveliness and humour well-matched to positive Leonians, though Gemini can be a little too flighty for Leo's underlying desire for security. Home-loving Cancerians and self-effacing Librans make excellent partners for Leos: Cancer provides the good home a Leo will love and submits quietly to Leo's dominating character; Libra is an affectionate and sociable type, able to share Leonian needs and desires without challenging the royal ego. The competitive instinct should be kept under control when a human Leonian meets the cat with pretensions to be King of the Beasts; there could be some spectacular clashes, but this is otherwise a specially good match.

Other signs should watch out for a few danger areas when considering whether to take on a little lion. The Sagittarian spirit of inquiry is well appreciated by human Leos and these two can make highly compatible travelling companions, but this opportunity is only appealing to a Leo cat if it involves travelling in grand style and a complete absence of unpleasant interludes due to quarantine regulations. Capricornian reticence is certainly mismatched with Leonian flamboyance, while idealistic Pisces can be trampled under the more wilful and boisterous Leonian traits, although this is a creative and loving pairing. Some problems are only to be expected in any partnership between Leo and Taurus, both hopelessly intransigent at times; with meticulous Virgo, soon exasperated by a lazy Leo; and with Scorpio, whose power games are played out secretively while Leo prefers to stride straight through any opposition. Finally, Aquarians be warned, fiery Leos are attracted to Aquarius as they are to all Air signs, but are closet conventionalists and do not take kindly to the Aquarian need for change; ultimately a conflict will arise.

THE THEATRE CAT

The theatre offers few good parts for cats. It is difficult enough to persuade a cat to act, rather than react or overact, let alone rely on it to produce consistent performances seven or eight times a week. Writers and directors have generally found it unwise to include such an unstable element in a theatrical scenario. Nevertheless, occasionally it happens that a cat is born with the theatre in its blood and it cannot be stopped from seeking the limelight.

One such cat was born, in time-honoured custom, in a costume basket behind the stage; as it happened, during the tempest scene in *King Lear*. The audience gasped and cowered on that close, thundery August night as the dramatic effect of the tempest was unleashed. So it was that at this thrillingly theatrical moment a tiny kitten made his first and most important début and in those opening minutes of his life absorbed the dynamic stage atmosphere. The first sound that he consciously registered was the audience's applause.

Within weeks, the furry bundle had acquired extraordinary ambitions to become a celebrated actor. Instant stardom was his goal; he had no intention of serving a long apprenticeship of the spear-carrying variety. To move his career into a classical vein, the kitten kept his ears and eyes open at rehearsals and began to plot impromptu appearances which would win him the attention of audience and critics. Shakespeare's famous stage direction 'Exit, pursued by a bear' gained a novel element from his intervention; more than once, the appearance of the ghost of Hamlet's father was announced by an eerie mewing in the traps below the stage; the growing cat frequently attended the Macbeths' grisly banquet, completely upstaging the dead Banquo's scheduled manifestation whenever possible; he also contributed a bold feline presence on the field at Agincourt, and was once borne triumphantly on stage clinging to the humpback of Richard III.

As a Leo, the cat was a self-confident and extrovert character. He might have done very well in movies, where any unhappy irrelevancies which had crept into his performance could be safely left on the cutting-room floor. But even had offers been pouring in thick and fast from Hollywood, this dedicated thespian would not have been easily tempted. His spirit was connected to the old tradition of the actor-manager. He wanted nothing more than to strut and fret his hour upon the stage; his lifeblood was daily contact with an admiring audience and the passions and intrigues of the close-knit company of actors. First night nerves and last night celebrations were the markers of his existence.

The theatre cat was undoubtedly a born performer. Despite his classical aspirations, some of his greatest successes were gained in revue and pantomime, where an unexpected talent for high comedy was revealed and his unique sense of timing contributed a wonderfully entertaining atmosphere of organized chaos. Audiences showed themselves deeply appreciative of his skills in these areas, and he became a real box-office draw. This was recognized by the canny theatre management, and finally the cat was allowed to ascend to a leading role – in an adaptation of Colette's *The Cat*, specially written for him by the theatre's resident playwright. The fact that he was playing against type in this saga – Colette's original being female – worried him not a bit, and his sensitivity to this difficult aspect of his performance was singled out for critical praise.

This is so far the crowning glory of his illustrious theatrical career, duly acknowledged by the mounting of his portrait in the theatre foyer alongside those of many other notable stage stars in whose company he now feels quite at home. A season of revivals is planned, and he hopes to go from strength to strength. Meanwhile, with typical generosity, he keeps an eye out for a worthy young successor capable of being schooled in this fine feline's actorly tradition.

VIRGO

24TH AUGUST – 23RD SEPTEMBER

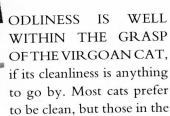

ODLINESS IS WELL WITHIN THE GRASP OF THE VIRGOAN CAT, if its cleanliness is anything to go by. Most cats prefer to be clean, but those in the sign of Virgo can positively make a career out of it. A full wash down twice a day, with in-between attention to paws and whiskers, is not excessive behaviour for such a cat; and if you venture within range as the Virgoan reaches the end of its cleansing routine, do not be surprised if your own paws are judged to be in need of a good wash. Keep a careful eye on a nursing queen with this Virgoan trait: she will lick her kittens clean so vigorously that they may feel they have suffered the equivalent of a full washing machine cycle, emerging sparkling but definitely dizzy.

Unsurprisingly, the bathroom is a favourite haunt of the Virgo not, as with Pisces, for its aquatic possibilities but simply because it is the sacred place of cleanliness. Install a wicker chair and some pretty cotton-covered cushions to give the cat a place to settle; it won't meddle with the bathroom accessories or teach itself to turn on the taps, but it will expect the room to have a freshness that matches its own high standards.

A parallel obsession for the Virgoan is its health. Hypochondria is a distinct possibility, but even the most minor ailment is a serious matter to the Virgo cat, the only representative of its species which actually enjoys a visit to the vet; that trip in the basket and the assorted smells of the waiting room signify that its complaints are being treated with proper gravity. There can be no cat which would willingly invite the indignity of having its temperature taken, but the Virgoan undergoes all other investigations with surprising equanimity. It should be possible, too, to administer a course of tablets without that usual terrible struggle which ends with the cat calmly walking three steps and spitting out the unswallowed pill. Virgoans are the cats for whom the palatable tablet is the greatest concept since pet foods were patented; they have been known to crunch up all sorts of remedies as if they were some kind of treat.

The fastidiousness of Virgo, which under the wrong influences can develop into an irritating finickiness, exists within one of the most independent characters in the Zodiac. The Virgoan is an intelligent and self-contained type, a cat with its own business to attend to, who comes and goes purposefully, and maintains a pleasant social manner while avoiding intense involvement. It normally presents a rather cool demeanour which preserves its sense of personal space and masks its underlying insecurity. It takes a long time to make friends and is a very analytical type. When first brought home, the Virgoan kitten will observe you quizzically, wondering what it is you have to offer. In this early stage of existence it delights to tease, and will test you out in all sorts of ways before consenting to rub along with you in a companionable way. It will go through the ritual of leaving a trail of muddy pawprints every time there is rain to make sure that you have the proper attitude to cleaning. Nothing less will do than that tiles shall be scrubbed and carpets vacuumed until they are humming with cleanliness.

Virgoans are empiricists to whom seeing is believing. Only when regular meals have turned up a sufficient number of times to make it a mathematical probability that the situation will continue does the feline Virgo relax and take for granted the relationship with its provider. It is possessed of a basic insecurity which underlies its need to be in control of its life. Though appreciative of communication, the Virgoan cat is not particularly demonstrative and certainly dislikes emotional scenes, whether over-the-top praise for its best behaviour or stupidly phrased blandishments intended to make it pay attention to you. Nevertheless, it does need to be enticed into showing its affection, but this must be so subtly performed as to be almost incidental.

Being a conscientious, responsible and independent type, the Virgoan cat is the perfect partner for a busy career person who is out of the house much of the time. As a matter of kindness and courtesy, it will appreciate being given agreeable surroundings in which to spend its hours alone. Natural materials (scrupulously clean, of course) make suitable furnishings for the Virgoan, and to maintain a fresh atmosphere, provide a few beautiful foliage plants which it can muse upon at leisure. Virgos are active cats, however, and will enjoy a well-designed garden in which to roam. They also have a modicum of adventurousness in their inner beings which appreciates new sights and sounds. It is a good idea to train the Virgoan cat from an early age to take short trips in the car and accompany you on outings and weekend vacations in the countryside, to provide a refreshing and stimulating break in the normal pattern of daily life.

The outdoor Virgoan maintains its personal distance from neighbouring felines as it does from the humans within the home. It abhors the idea of being goaded into excessive behaviour, and would prefer not to fight or to become involved in public mating rituals. Its sense of order is somewhat distressed by the anarchic behaviour which can arise among unrestrained felines, so it will certainly spend some time studying the comings and goings of other cats, to work out the social structure in its immediate vicinity. The Virgoan cat will then select the pathways and resting places which it can use day-to-day without inviting unwelcome attention.

It is difficult to say who is the ideal friend and protector of the Virgoan cat. This is not because Virgos are especially demanding, but they have a discreet sense of themselves which should not be challenged by insensitive communication from outside. Gemini is perhaps the best companion for Virgo, capable of an intelligent exchange of feelings but sufficiently active and independent on its own account to command respect from a Virgoan. Scorpio, too, stands in the realm of good communications, but may have a mischievous desire to explore a seamier side of life which is anathema to the fastidious Virgoan. The Piscean fantasy world bounces off the back of Virgoan common sense without damaging either party's sense of self and the combination can produce an amiable blend of reality and possibility. Investiga-tive Sagittarians, if not averse to company, can take along a Virgo on their travels whose insatiable curiosity matches their own, though the drawback here, as with Scorpio, is an occasional Sagittarian tendency to be slovenly about the house, clashing with the Virgoan desire for spotless surroundings.

It might seem that another houseproud Virgo should be a perfect host to a Virgoan cat, but these two have an air of disinterestedness which can cause them to disconnect on every level. Better a painstaking Libran who can put up with any demand from a loved one; it is important, however, that this pairing includes a relatively easygoing Virgo who does not appear to treat sensitive Libra with disdain.

DICK WHITTINGTON'S CAT

*V*irgos show a talent for service which they are able to exercise with no loss of personal dignity, so it is not surprising to find that a cat legendary for making the fortune of its master was indeed a Virgoan. The cat's success in orchestrating the spectacular improvement in her own and her master's situations was due to her typically Virgoan desire for clean surroundings, which in this case reaped extraordinary rewards.

At the time of Dick Whittington's meeting with the Virgoan cat, Dick was in the employment of a rich merchant named Fitzwarren. Alone in a cold attic swarming with rats and mice, it soon occurred to Dick to find a cat, who would be company and at the same time would eradicate the vermin. At the market one day, he spotted the Virgoan cat sitting in the capacious basket of her present keeper, a kind person who had brought the cat on a day trip as a break from her busy activity as a mouser. Dick approached this woman and offered to buy the cat for the single penny which he had in his pocket. The woman was reluctant to part with the pleasant and useful animal, and for such a small sum, but she took pity on Dick's obviously lonely and impoverished state, and finally agreed to the sale.

The cat was an unsentimental soul who thought nothing of being suddenly acquired by a different owner, but on the return to Dick's rat-filled attic, her fastidious Virgoan feelings were appalled by the miserable conditions. As much for her own benefit as for Dick's, she set to work immediately on chasing the rats and mice and within days had completely cleared the place of the unwelcome rodents. Dick showed his appreciation by regularly cleaning the room thoroughly and using his meagre income to buy a pretty cushion for the cat to sleep on.

They lived companionably together in the attic for some time, until Dick was reluctantly obliged to send his cat as merchandise on Mr Fitzwarren's trading expedition. The Virgoan turned out to be an excellent ship's cat, quickly becoming a favourite of the rough and ready sailors who admired her independent ways, and she set about catching rats just as effectively as she had in Dick's small attic.

After many weeks, the ship docked in the port of a rich eastern country, and the ship's captain was invited to a special banquet at the palace of the king. Before they could eat, the food was attacked and largely carried off by a massive army of rats.

His faculties sharpened by hunger, the captain immediately offered the services of Dick's cat who set to work with all speed, ashamed that such obviously affluent surroundings should be afflicted with filthy vermin. It was generally assumed that the cat's enthusiasm for the task sprang solely from obedience to a natural feline instinct and not, as was in fact the case, from the innate Virgoan desire for a spotless environment.

Interest in the story usually ends with the vast treasure of gold and jewels paid by the grateful king being returned to Dick Whittington in London, but accounts vary as to the subsequent fate of Dick's cat. Some reports state that the cat stayed where she was and became a close confidante of the eastern king, who relied on her honest and coolly analytical character to support him in

his often difficult position as Head of State. An alternative version holds that she was returned to Dick Whittington's new riverside mansion in London and assisted him during his mayoral terms of office. In both histories, it is clear that the cat became well loved, respected and celebrated, and acquired an active and interesting life. Her private and public business, to her highest delight and in contrast to the early days in the miserable attic, was ever after carried out in comfortable and pristine surroundings.

LIBRA

24TH SEPTEMBER – 23RD OCTOBER

OUNT UP ALL THE MANY POSITIVE ASPECTS OF LIBRA and the answer seems to be the perfect cat – intelligent, charming, lovable and loving, a bringer of peace and harmony. Librans are possessed of a well-developed aesthetic sense and can be relied upon to appreciate the decorative aspects of their surroundings. Clean, bright rooms discreetly ornamented with beautiful fabrics and generous flower arrangements delight the Libran love of luxury. Scents are important, too; the theory that cats enjoy perfumes for their own sake could surely have been tested and proven by a Libran target group. And an exquisite environment is a compliment fully reciprocated by the Libran cat, whose agenda invariably includes a daily washing routine which might well last, with occasional diversions, from morning until night. Bright eyes, glossy fur and immaculate paws are minimum personal requirements (although for the Libran, tidiness does not

rate equally with cleanliness as a desirable asset).

Pampering is never lost on a Libran, whose main aim in life is to be adored and who is only too aware that love and encouragement work both ways. It is willing to provide plenty of flattery and attention in order to receive the same in return. This tasteful, delicate creature may be found attractively arranged among the pot-plants on your windowsill, waiting to greet you when you return home. As soon as it hears your key in the door it is at your feet purring and rubbing affectionately. The Libran continually uses close contact as the most flattering expression of love. A quiet evening listening to music or watching television is the Libran cat's idea of heaven; it will settle upon you while you are captive in your chair, and for you this should be the end of any activity more strenuous than fondling the cat's ears or stroking its paws for the remainder of the evening.

If you hold strong views on not allowing a cat to sleep on your bed, either avoid taking on a Libran or get a padlock for the bedroom door, because the bedroom is the special province of this sign. Feline Librans need only half a chance to make themselves comfortable on top of the eiderdown, under the duvet, between the blankets – whatever the style of your soft furnishings, every cat born under Libra understands the comforting properties of bedlinen, but generously consents that you should share the pleasure. Fortunately, another aspect of Libra appreciates old-fashioned concepts such as good manners, so the cat may be persuaded to leave the guest bedroom alone, at least when a guest is actually occupying it.

Librans hate to embarrass or contradict anyone and need extra sensitivity from their friends. This is one of the few cats that will try to eat a food it doesn't really fancy in order to please – if it thinks the food is your special choice – and play endless boring games of catch with anything from a screwed-up piece of paper to a catnip mouse – if it imagines that this is your favourite pastime. This eventually becomes depressing to even the most accommodating of cats, so be on the alert for any hint of suffering.

So far, there are few intimations that a Libran can be a tiresome prospect, but imagine all this sweetness and light taken to extremes. Libra's very willingness to please can become a terrible burden to a close companion – the doormat tendency occasionally comes uppermost and the Libran will long to lay down his or her life for you whether you like it or not. Furthermore, this is a sign which sets very high standards and suffers appalling disappointment when these are not met.

Martyrdom of one kind or another often appeals to Libra, whether this involves putting up with selfishness or sluttishness in others, or failing itself by not fulfilling cherished ambitions. Under the sign of the Scales, life can go out of control once the balance is upset.

A suffering, depressed or guilty Libran is as problematic as a cat can be. Indeed, there is a clear possibility of an actual neurosis developing, with retreat or paranoia being Libran's likely response if a sorry situation goes unchecked. A retreating Libran is extremely inventive in finding places to hide – so check out any cavities that exist in your home, whether up the chimney or at the back of the washing machine. A paranoid cat is a seriously alarming housemate; far from rubbing affectionately against your ankles, it may dash out to butt its head against your shoe and then flee for its life. While you puzzle over this strange event, the cat interprets the interlude as follows: that it came up to greet you and you kicked it without warning or provocation. Such behaviour must be nipped in the bud by means of much loving attention and all sorts of special treats. Otherwise, the paranoia may turn out to be a self-fulfilling prophecy as you become more and more exasperated with the cat's unlovable histrionics.

Librans can be quite devoted homebodies, so there should not be excessive night prowling, and they will probably avoid confrontations in the mini-jungle outdoors as aggression is not a notable element of the Libran character. A fresh-air Libran is most likely to be seen sitting in the centre of a patch of grass and gazing up at the sky. This does not signify an ongoing interest in astrophysics, however intelligent the cat. The reason for this still, attentive pose is more easily defined: soft blues and greens are the special Libra colours, abundantly supplied by nature on clement days when the sky is clear. The cat is literally taking a refresher course, feeding its senses and its soul.

Outdoors can be baffling to the Libran, especially where territorial disputes are concerned. Another often negative side to Libra is a terrible indecisiveness, due to its being able to see both sides of a question, and a few more facets that no one else has recognized. Laziness can also be a specifically Libran attribute, so squabbling over terrain is not only offensive but an unnecessary exertion. The Libran cat will prefer to establish a small patch of its own, radiating from the catflap, where ownership rights cannot be in dispute and the amenities can be enjoyed at leisure.

Librans are good companions for almost everyone. This is an adaptable sign that can accommodate the domesticity of a Cancerian or the conservatism of a Capricorn and equally complement the extroversion of Aries and Leo. The solid reassurance of the Taurean character is a perfect haven for occasionally anxious Librans, but other signs not notable for craving comfort and security can be good for Libra in other ways – Gemini and Scorpio are two that can draw out the active and unusual properties of the Libran mind.

A danger area for Librans is the tendency to submerge themselves under the influence of more powerfully directed personalities. Therefore, if the negative characteristics of their companions come uppermost, the Libran balance is destroyed with inevitably unhappy results. Otherwise, Libra is a sociable and genuinely tolerant sign with a yearning for pleasant pairings.

THE PHILOSOPHER CAT

Anyone who has spent any time around cats is familiar with those periods of intense brooding which a cat will have, when it sits settled squarely on its haunches with its half-closed eyes fixed upon a point of mysterious interest a short distance ahead. Often the creature looks as if it has the weight of the world upon its shoulders – 24 hours to solve a crisis, perhaps, or to provide a definitive answer to what lies at the edge of the Universe. Unsympathetic people have claimed that a cat's mind is either a comforting blank, or that it can only focus on the question of where the next meal is coming from. Cat lovers know that, on the contrary, a brooding cat is certainly lost in profound thought. But thought about what?

If it is a Libran cat, it is probably engaged in abstract problems and intellectual self-debate. The charming manner and accommodating character of a Libran can mask a powerful intelligence normally underexercised by its social circumstances, hence the periods of solitary engagement when there are no other claims on the cat's time. This activity also gives it the opportunity to make a virtue of its Libran indecisiveness, in that seeing both sides of a point is an absolute necessity when the argument is with oneself.

One such Libran started early on its philosophical career, being an observant type which soon noticed that most things seemed to have a purpose. Bees, for example, make honey, and cows give milk. People are constantly making off in different directions carrying briefcases or shopping baskets of which the contents clearly make an important contribution to the daily round. So far, so good, but when the cat came to ponder what might be the purpose of a domestic cat, nothing much seemed to come to mind.

Being blissfully unaware of such great predecessors as Descartes, Bishop Berkeley or Jean-Paul Sartre, the cat set out all over again to puzzle on the nature of existence and, most specifically, that of cats. After much mental tussling, it came up with a rather satisfying proposition phrased thus: 'I eat, therefore I am'. This seemed pretty profound, as did the concomitant proposal, 'I sleep, therefore I am'. In fact, perhaps that one was even better, as waking up must surely be a proof of existence. If one was basically non-existent, it would be possible to vanish during sleep; or would it?

Naturally this posed the question of an internal or external view of existence. This came up in rather more conventional terms, as in '*Esse est percipi*', 'To be is to be perceived'. So, is a cat really there if no one is paying it any attention? The philosopher cat found it easier to apply this precept to dogs, who were self-evidently super-fluous elements with a duty to disappear if no one wanted to look at them.

Slowly but surely, it was making its way towards the theory that cats possess something beyond the simple fact of being. This it described to itself as a kind of essence of catness, a quality not even

understood by cats because to define it, even privately, would be to diminish its quality. Nevertheless, this did not rule out the question of whether one had to exist in order to acquire this essence; or did the essence itself tend to materialize a form which it might inhabit? Could something be real which could not be defined? The questions seemed to multiply.

So far from being depressed by these ever-increasing suppositions, the cat was greatly stimulated and woke from its frequent periods of sleep eager to get on with unravelling the difficult thoughts. It had thus proved, quite without meaning to, the Aristotelian proposition that pure reasoning is a source of happiness and, almost incidentally, had supplied itself with a lifelong purpose, which it still pursues.

SCORPIO

24TH OCTOBER – 22ND NOVEMBER

CORPIO IS THE SIGN THAT SIGNALS GREAT INTENSITY OF FEELING, though its outer image may be perfectly cool and calm. Stirrings on the underside of life are fascinating to Scorpios and this is a sign which can produce magicians, spies or power-brokers, the great manipulators behind the scenes. It can also include an element of the macabre; think of all those horror movies and thrillers in which a cat stalks through the background to the action and always turns up as the tension increases – wandering the graveyard at midnight or silently guarding the body on the library floor. The Scorpio cat is the perfect model for this elusive character, a brooding presence which may be a dark angel or a malignant devil.

This is a feeling that you will definitely get if you share your life with a feline Scorpio. This cat is an enigma for whom concealment, physical or mental, is a fine art, but you will find its influence everywhere. When you are sitting in your living room quietly enjoying a cup of coffee and reading a magazine, you will get that sudden sensation of being watched that causes a nameless anxiety to rise in the pit of your stomach. Looking around, you will discover that the cat has silently tucked itself into an unobtrusive vantage point, and is staring as intently as only a cat can do. Who knows what it wants, but its eyes seem to penetrate your outer disguises and inner desires. You must simply be grateful that the Scorpio cat by nature keeps your secrets as it keeps its own.

Whether you can strike a successful relationship with a Scorpio depends entirely on you. These are not the kind of cats which make concessions; they expect the compromises to be on your side. If you are looking for a cheerful, outgoing companion, get yourself an Aries or a Leo. Even the most relaxed Scorpio (possibly a contradiction in terms) will leave you wondering where you stand. A negative character in this sign can be jealous, vindictive and vengeful, the very antithesis of the fireside friend. A single incident which puts you in the cat's black books will never be forgiven or forgotten: if you tread on its tail, however accidentally, or leave it unfed overnight when a dire emergency crops up elsewhere, you may as well call it a day with the Scorpio cat and lose no time in finding it a good home to go to. Scorpio does a fine line in nursing a grievance and if it seriously turns against you, that's for life.

If you are still contemplating living with a Scorpio cat this must be because the dark side of Scorpio has its own fascination. But it must be said that not all is darkness and despair, however occult the cat's behaviour. Scorpio is a sincere friend provided nothing happens to turn the tide of friendship and, perhaps surprisingly, can be an intensely home-loving type when conditions are to its liking. Scorpios enjoy close company and good food and the Scorpio cat will respond to softness in its surroundings, if not in the behaviour of its housemates. Furnish your home with many dimly lit, draped alcoves and the cat will be in seventh heaven. Lush curtains are a particular

delight and the cat will soon investigate all the possibilities for living in and around their folds and hollows. Beautiful beds are also appreciated: a heavily draped four-poster, of course, is the ideal. The kitchen is another area of particular interest to the Scorpio; the cat perhaps imagines your cooking to be some highly advanced form of domestic alchemy and will furtively examine every ingredient and utensil that you use, looking for its special power.

Although an established home is important, Scorpios have the ability to make a complete break with the pattern of their lives. If you are moving across town, across the country, or around the world, a Scorpio cat is the one most

likely to resettle without regret into a whole new manner of existence. Those touching sagas of cats which trek across continents to catch up with their owners do not suggest a Scorpio in the starring role. Whether you take the cat with you or leave it behind, the Scorpio does not merely adjust, it wipes out the past and starts over. If one day you pass your old home where a Scorpio cat was handed over to a sympathetic neighbour, don't waste your time making a sentimental visit bearing parcels of kitty-treats: the cat never saw you before in its life.

Out in the cat community, Scorpio is the cat that walks by itself. Other cats may be wary of it because it is a magnetic but untouchable personality, baffling to less powerful feline souls. Scorpios do not, however, like to be challenged, so the stout-hearted among its immediate neighbours will not get the satisfaction of a direct confrontation. The cat is in the business of manipulation, engineering a situation to its own requirements whenever possible.

The Scorpio cat takes a secret pleasure in slumming, and the most well-fed and well-cared-for town cat is occasionally to be seen scavenging among dustbins to select from their repulsive treasures. This is a form of recreation for a cat which otherwise finds relaxation a chore. Distinctive atmospheres also appeal to Scorpios: cats which prowl churchyards and curl up on accommodating gravestones are not a movie director's fantasy; they are, without doubt, Scorpios taking their ease.

If you have a restless or knotted-up Scorpio cat, dig a hole in the garden and sink a small pool, to give the cat a pleasant recreation area where it can unwind. To save on high fish mortality rates, install some interesting aquatic plants rather than a fleet of shimmering goldfish. The cat can get as much pleasure from scooping up a tangle of waterlily runners as it can from catching fish which it does not need to eat. Despite their self-contained poise, Scorpios have plenty of suppressed energy which needs to be given an outlet.

The best type of person to share a home with a Scorpio cat is one strong enough to absorb Scorpionian intensity and respect the cat's subterranean private live. The other two Water signs bond well with Scorpio – Cancer, sharing the need for a secure home and offering equal loyalty in friendship; and Pisces, a sign of great sensitivity which in auspicious circumstances is perfectly tuned to similar aspects of Scorpio. Capricorns, though an aura of magic is rarely their talent, have a serious outlook on life which Scorpios find sympathetic. A Libran is likely to be able to appreciate a Scorpio, provided the dark side is not uppermost, which would unsettle the more peaceable character of Libra. Taurus is a more physical sign than Scorpio, but it is the Zodiacal opposite and these are partnerships which very often work out well: Taurus and Scorpio are both remarkable for their fixity, and though they may have different dreams and desires, they share the need for a solidly based relationship on which to build their lives.

THE VATICAN CAT

Centuries ago, when the nation-states of Europe were constantly at war, the Vatican in Rome wielded considerable political power. The Pope and his officials made it their business to chart the shifting patterns of treaties, alliances and conflicts between the states and to manipulate the political intrigues.

A silent witness to the comings and goings of the politicians was a slim, sleek cat, an enigmatic presence with her hooded eyes and sinuous tail. This cat had thoroughly absorbed the conspiratorial atmosphere and trusted no one. She was a favourite of the Pope, however, and knowing him to be someone apart from all the rest, she responded to his favours and made the most of her privileged position. Many people at the papal court were superstitiously afraid of her, and those who knew she was a Scorpio suspected her of having secret power and possibly of communing with the forces of darkness. Ignoring such foolishness, the cat made her way through the court unimpeded and mostly alone. She loved the dark corners and shadowed corridors of the palace, the rich furnishings and gold ornament of the ceremonial chambers, and the swirling colours of the officials' robes.

The cat was, in fact, privy to the highly sensitive political negotiations conducted in the Pope's inner chambers. She had a hiding place in the vast sleeve of the Pope's robe, from where she spied upon the visiting dignitaries and followed the sometimes angry, sometimes conciliatory tones of the negotiations.

It was through this privilege that she unwittingly caused a serious incident which had the most violent repercussions. An alliance was to be arranged between two of the most powerful warring states, signified by an important marriage ceremony which was to be conducted by the Pope. Part of the marriage settlement was the largest ruby ever seen, a sumptuous jewel set in gold which would be handed over as the final symbol of the signed treaty of alliance. The Pope had requested to see this important object prior to the marriage. As the glistening jewel was presented to him, the cat shifted her position under his robe and her sleek head momentarily appeared by the hem of his sleeve.

She had never seen anything so beautiful, even in all the treasures around her. The ruby seemed to wink and sparkle enticingly: in that moment she conceived a passion to make it her own.

The jewel was well guarded, but no one could think it necessary to protect it from the attentions of a cat. In the dead of night, the cat made her way to the chamber where the ruby was kept in a special box, hidden in a niche in the wall. She started quietly to fiddle with the gold catch on the box until eventually her stealth and patience were rewarded and the catch slipped free. Tipping up the lid she snatched the jewel from its cushion and without hesitation bore it away to a secret hiding place known only to herself.

All hell broke loose next day when the loss of the ruby was discovered. The parties to the alliance both departed quickly and in anger, and war between their countries was resumed to devastating effect. The papal court was thoroughly disrupted. The atmosphere of secrecy and mistrust seemed to increase daily, as the mystery of the missing jewel remained unsolved.

The cat never gave away her secret and spent hours brooding pleasurably on her treasure, oblivious to the havoc she had caused. Those few who suspected the truth, though for the wrong reasons, made her life at the court more precarious, but none could produce an accusation. She lived, in fact, to a ripe old age and saw the downfall of many of her enemies. Rumour has it, to this day, that the ruby remains in her secret cache, unseen ever since by human eye.

SAGITTARIUS

23rd November – 21st December

IVELY SAGITTARIANS CAN SEVERELY TEST THE THEORY THAT A CAT HAS NINE LIVES. Being life's natural explorers and travellers, they are constantly on the move, boldly going where no cat has been before. All well and good, as cats are known to be swift, sure-footed creatures with a certain instinct for danger and quick reaction to a crisis. The trouble is, Sagittarian cats are often the exception to this rule. They have been known to break with the feline tradition of grace under pressure and make colossal misjudgements. The sad truth is that the Sagittarian is a clumsy cat: spying an interesting corner at the top of the bookshelves – perhaps the entrance to a secret passage? – it leaps towards its goal, scattering your prize ornaments all over the floor; sailing through the air towards what looks like the perfect mossy landing pad, the cat realizes too late that this is an algae-covered rainwater barrel. You will need nerves of steel to observe the comings and goings of a Sagittarian, but fortunately for the cat, its occasionally misguided adventurousness is accompanied by an optimistic and philosophical temperament.

There is no point in trying to curb the roving nature of the Sagittarian. Coop it up in a high-rise apartment and in between leaving a trail of havoc through every room, the cat will miss no opportunity to try to launch itself from the window, even if this is open just the merest crack. The best environment for a Sagittarian cat is one which gives it free and full scope to investigate the lie of the land. In the country it will trek for miles, evolving complex stories in its head of its intrepid doings. If you visit the local market and see something very like your cat darting in and out of the busy stalls and hobnobbing with the natives, don't dismiss this as a coincidence just because you know your cat was last seen at home washing its paws on a sunny windowsill. The cat certainly knows a shortcut or two which has beaten you to the finishing line, and any opportunity of getting to know the customs of a new environment, the further from home the better, is right up its alley.

You may find that the cat brings home souvenirs of its travels – a fresh fish or a piece of pretty ribbon are equally appropriate evidence of its market trip; it will fetch down a bird's nest from the highest tree in the neighbourhood or spend hours digging ancient cup-handles out of the flowerbeds with the enthusiasm of the born archaeologist.

Gifts from the Sagittarian cat are a major sign of its affection, and there may be few others signalled by this unsentimental soul. It is exceptionally cheering company but not given to providing a soft shoulder to cry on; its love is shown in practical ways and it is pleased by a reciprocal arrangement. If you wield the can-opener once or twice a day, the Sagittarian cat is assured of your caring intentions, and an acknowledgement is as good as an endearment to this animal, which is too busy to stop for a long heart-to-heart session. It will enjoy sharing in your own activities provided these are creative and purposeful. If you have a workshop or studio full of interesting devices, the cat will be pleased to investigate all the possibilities – but remember this is not a neat or careful cat; keep sharp tools well out of the way and be prepared for an impromptu masterpiece when the cat inadvertently dips its paws in your paint palette.

Sagittarius is a sporty type, however, and prefers to commune with the great outdoors whenever possible. If there is a long garden path, the cat will vigorously practise sprinting and even hurdling; it will climb walls, trees and drainpipes wherever there is a foothold. It is rarely distracted from its personal pursuits by the demands of neighbourhood politics; this is a free and independent soul with no great desire to join the local cat-club. It delights in the chase but is less interested in the catch, so its engagements with local felines, male and female, are usually brief.

Sagittarian adventurousness is inborn; it is never too early to start training a kitten of this sign to enjoy car travel and regular vacationing. Ideally, the cat wishes to discover new sights, sounds and activities, so it is possible to take a city cat to the country for a change of air, or vice versa. Make sure it has some familiar possessions in either place which enable it to identify and return to home-base whenever necessary. Otherwise you may lose track of it and it will end up a vagabond cat, wary of any fixed situation and exhibiting a highly developed talent for petty theft to keep itself alive.

Sagittarians are less sleepy than some other cats, and a change is often as good as a rest. The cat will recline among luxurious furnishings considering the possibilities for its next adventure, but rare signs of laziness in a Sagittarian should be carefully watched. It may be tempted into an excess of eating and relaxation if it has had a particularly busy and demanding time, but self-indulgence is not a talent of Sagittarians. Nine times out of ten, the cat gets itself on the move again before idleness becomes a habit, but if not it needs to be pushed back into action or a flabby and unsatisfied creature will be the result.

Two main attributes qualify you to be the keeper of a free-ranging Sagittarian tiger: an outgoing personality – shrinking violets will feel they are constantly being trodden under the feet of the vigorous Sagittarian – and a fairly well-developed sense of humour which enables you to see the funny side of a succession of minor disasters. Inquisitive Aquarians and fun-loving Arians will have no trouble in absorbing the odder outcomes of Sagittarian blundering; both are equipped with a view of life which enjoys the active participation of Sagittarius for good or ill. Geminis, too, are enlivened by a companion with plenty to do on its own account and are generally busy enough with their own interests not to be disrupted by the occasional crashing noises which indicate a Sagittarian at play. Boldly energetic Leos share these qualities with Sagittarians. The only danger area here is that a Leo who is mainly bluster may be unmasked by a well-meaning Sagittarian; these cats can drop a heavy paw on a person's weakest spot without any intention to be unkind.

Signs with greater sensitivity to the psychological pitfalls of close relationships may shrink from the straightforwardness of Sagittarius. Librans and Pisceans, though natural candidates for pairings, may be looking for a quieter life than the Sagittarian is likely to provide. On the home front, domesticated Cancerians can shrink into their shells at the sight of a Sagittarian making its way across the living room without touching ground. Taureans, too, who love their possessions, may feel themselves occasionally in conflict with a scarcely houseproud Sagittarian cat.

CHIPANGO, THE DISCOVERER

With the world now rigorously mapped and the shape of the continents so familiar, no modern cat could look forward to an adventure equal to that of the cat that sailed with Columbus. This of course was a Sagittarian, one of the natural voyagers of the Zodiac temperamentally equipped to discover new worlds.

It is difficult now to appreciate the ambition and courage of the early navigators. Selecting from the limited knowledge available to him, Columbus planned his great voyage of discovery to take him from Europe to the Far East, to China and Japan via a western route. For his crew, the journey would be a greater act of faith, as no one had yet proved the theory that the world was round, or that the lands of the east could be approached via the west.

The voyage was planned, the ship stocked and standing ready at the port. The addition of a Sagittarian cat as crew member seems to have been a minor unplanned element, caused by the animal taking a hasty detour up the gangplank while being chased by an irate fishmonger. By the time the cat ventured from its hiding place to make sure the coast was clear, the ship had sailed.

To the cat's amazement, day by day the coast became even clearer. Fortunately its adventurous spirit was intrigued rather than dismayed by this strange occurrence. It was soon adopted by some of the low-ranking seamen and given a minimal diet and some friendly attention in return for performing a few useful tasks, such as mousing in the grainstore and, more excitingly, keeping company with the sailor assigned to the lonely lookout post. The cat was commonly called Chipango, after the island of Japan toward which the tiny fleet was aimed.

From the forecastle, the cat saw some of the more spectacular sights of the voyage: colourful sunsets, leaping dolphins and the strange sea of sargasso, like a golden cornfield blanketing the ocean. After days of sailing without sight of land, even Columbus was growing uncertain of his calculations, and a move was afoot to try to make him change course. At this point, Chipango started an anxious chattering brought on by huge flocks of birds passing over the ship. It was decided to use the birds as an aid to navigation and Columbus altered course to the southwest. Chipango was again present with the lookout when, within a few days, land was sighted.

The ships were of course in the Bahamas, although Columbus clung to the theory that they had come close to the land mass of Asia. Chipango watched the strange flora and fauna with fascination, and sampled the exotic foods given to the crew by friendly islanders. Realizing the importance of keeping contact with the ship, on its occasional trips ashore the cat was content to remain tucked into the coat of a seaman, and resisted the temptation to leave its vantage point and run free into the undergrowth bordering the settled areas of the island coast.

After the relative calm of the outward voyage, however, exciting and dangerous events were still in store. The *Santa Maria*, Columbus's flagship, was grounded on a coral reef; all hands were saved, but it proved a highly anxious moment for Chipango, who was gathered up at the last minute and conveyed in safety to one of the sister ships. The return to Europe, too, was an eventful period due to days and nights of storms. Through the

worst, the cat crawled into an empty barrel and clung grimly to the sides until the ship's motion lost its violence.

It is not a cat's business to be fêted as a discoverer, nor was this canny Sagittarian concerned with the politics of trade and territory which so interested Columbus and his colleagues. On arrival at his home port, Chipango recognized the sights and smells of his former environment, and slipped off the ship. He made his way to old haunts where new adventures beckoned, carrying with him his secret superior knowledge of the world and a new name with which to sail the seas.

CAPRICORN

FROM THE SIGN OF THE GOAT COME MANY OF LIFE'S MOST SOLID CITIZENS and a cat born under Capricorn can be a most excellent companion. The behaviour of a Capricorn is rarely wilful or excessive, but the Capricornian personality carries a strong if well-guarded sense of self, and the element of deliberation can be seen in its actions even where specific motives are not immediately apparent.

Outwardly even-tempered and self-contained, the Capricornian cherishes submerged ambitions which you are expected to fulfil on his or her behalf, and will demonstrate a well-developed talent for subtle expressions of disappointment if these expectations are not met. So you may be delighted with the damp basement that represents your first independent home, but you will find your feline friend washing fastidiously on every occasion and lifting its paws disgustedly as it crosses the carpet. Such behaviour is designed to make you feel guilty, and to make sure you realize that this cat has no intention of becoming accustomed to such unsatisfactory arrangements. An elegantly proportioned town house or a spacious and comfortable country cottage should be the cherished aim, and the sooner the better, although the Capricornian has the patience to work slowly towards a really desirable goal.

Even as the situation improves, there is no home so clean, comfortable and efficiently run that the Capricornian cannot find some tiny element falling below standard, but you may be excused from judgement as long as the cat can see the continuous efforts you are making to achieve perfection. And there are reciprocal benefits from this perfectionism for the person prepared to give a little more than house room to a Capricorn: a cat which takes such a critical interest in its surroundings does not make puddles on the carpet or claw the curtains to shreds.

The Capricorn's great expectations extend also to feeding arrangements. Capricornians prefer traditional food and will expect good, solid catfood to turn up promptly at dinner-time on every day of their lives. New-fangled meaty chunks, occasional vegetarian dishes or last-minute left-overs do not impress these cats. One compensation for the fact that you are expected to provide the best, whatever the circumstances, is that at least it is understood that you are entitled to the best as well. Unfortunately, the cat cannot take over as breadwinner, although if it could it would do a grand job. Capricornians are nothing if not hardworking, their unadvertised ambitions well served by a willingness to plod up the ladder rung by rung to success.

Capricorns are not the world's greatest socializers and will generally be content to spend a lot of time at home. No self-respecting Capricorn bothers to ingratiate itself with neighbourhood cats. Lacking overt aggression or a primary urge to conquer new territories, the Capricornian cat will pick its way disinterestedly through the minefield of local cat politics – no one's enemy and no one's ally.

Indoors the Capricorn cat gains a sense of security and it is a loyal and loving companion. This is not often openly demonstrated, and it will sometimes treat even the best of friends to the kind of disdainful stare that makes the recipient feel like something the cat brought in. You are well advised not to take this personally, however, as the Capricornian is a shy creature and cool or tactless behaviour may only be a mask for the inner uncertainties that it struggles with quietly day by day. This cat depends upon you more than you may realize; it appreciates a stable and friend-ly presence, though it is often unable to share its emotions.

The Capricornian tends towards hypochon-dria, and a clever cat makes the most of every ache and pain to obtain the degree of extra comfort and care which it undoubtedly feels should really be its permanent lot in life. Persistent limping with no sign of actual damage could be mere malingering, but it is worth providing the expected sympathy. Capricornian cats find it difficult to engage in affectionate behaviour and a feigned illness or injury could provide the rare chance for a pleasant cuddle: these somewhat inhibited cats need a reasonable excuse to become relaxed in company.

One key to understanding a Capricorn is to recognize a trait peculiar to this sign. Capricornians tend to live their lives backwards in relation to expected development; they have a second childhood in place of, rather than as well as, the first. This can be disconcerting to the uninformed human, not to say embarrassing when a person is determinedly attempting to start a game of 'Kitty See The Ball' under the solemn gaze of a Capricornian kitten. You can throw and catch the ball yourself, but no matter how enthusiastic your attentions, this kitten will make it plain that it would rather be doing something practical, such as eating, washing or watching the grass grow. Several years later, you will be caught out again when choosing a comfortable cat-bed for your pot-bellied old Goat to settle into through middle age. The Capricornian cat has by now just discovered the delights of chasing its own tail, flying after invisible prey, or unravelling knitting wool in order to wind it around the chair legs.

This is not to imply that a Capricornian cat offers only years of humourless companionship crowned by a burst of geriatric mania. Capricorns may insist sternly on adherence to particular goals and standards, but they have a grace and charm all of their own and in the right circumstances — given security and release from anxiety — are extraordinarily pleasant and amusing companions. Their brand of humour may be a little quirky, but once you have discovered how it works, you are in for an entertaining relationship all the better for being grounded on Capricorn's conscientiousness and loyalty.

Who is the ideal person to offer a home to the Capricornian cat? Surprisingly, although this sign has some definite and immutable characteristics, almost every other Zodiac sign can form a useful and rewarding bond with Capricorn. A Taurean, for example, finds a sympathetic note in the Capricornian desire for material comfort and security. Differences of temperament are compensated by a number of well-matched character traits. Cancerians are good for Capricorns for similar reasons: their nesting instincts are highly appealing to the Capricorn's need for settled circumstances.

A person born under Libra is an excellent friend for a Capricorn cat: Libran indecisiveness is complemented by Capricornian practicality, and there is a great potential for gentle attachment offering a high degree of mutual support. Capricorn and Gemini do well together under the rule that opposites attract, in a curiously successful blend of Geminian volatility and the cautious conventionalism of Capricorn.

The sign least suited to pairing with Capricorn is Leo, whose self-confidence and vigour can be overwhelming to the self-contained Capricornian character. In their turn, Leos are likely to become exasperated with the Capricornian need to find everything in its place and life progressing nicely on a step-by-step basis. These two are emotional opposites and it is probably not worth either of them making the effort to overcome the differences: both have much to offer and can readily find far more felicitous partnerships elsewhere in the Zodiac.

BARNEY, THE MILL CAT

Working windmills are now a thing of the past, but a number of mills remain standing, monuments to the period of industrial history when men and their machines laboured long to provide the bare necessities of daily life. But it was not only the human workers whose hard and incessant task it was to keep the business of the mill turning smoothly. The presence of a catflap at the base of the mill is often testimony to another kind of conscientious employee involved in the work.

One such busy mill cat was a Capricornian named Barney, a heavy cat with a somewhat gruff manner, who went about his work with silent efficiency. His mill stood in a flat area of countryside where the wind frequently blew strongly across the low terrain. Nevertheless, there were some days of calm when not so much as a breeze stirred the sails of the windmill. To folk in other occupations, these slow sunny days brought a pleasurable listlessness, but among the millers such times created a terrible tension that even Barney could feel.

The other major threat to the valuable function of the mill would be the rise of a plague of rats or mice, and it was Barney's responsibility to make sure that this threat never became a reality. To this end, much of his time was spent patrolling the circular ground floor of the mill, where the grain sacks were stored.

The mouse population was never allowed to grow large under Barney's vigilance, but neither did it seem ever to disappear completely. From time to time he pondered the baffling persistence of individual rodents which were emboldened to attack the sacks of grain. There always seemed to be one more poking its nose out of a tiny mousehole. With true Capricornian doggedness, Barney would chase off the offender before it could do any harm. His preferred tactic was to take the mouse by surprise, terrify it with his growling, and pursue it out of the mill and far off across the land. Unfortunately, for he was a well-fed and kindly cat, there was sometimes no option but to deal violently with these interfering opponents.

To his colleagues, Barney was known as a good mill cat and an effective mouser. They never found any tell-tale tears in the grain sacks where contamination could creep in or a quantity of the precious grain might spill out. Barney did a twice-daily round of the upper floors, as well as his duty in the storeroom. This enabled him to check for tiny intruders which might have scuttled unseen up the stairs, or climbed the pulley ropes to the weighing room. It was also a means of keeping in touch with all the workings of the mill, for he conscientiously liked to see a job through from start to finish.

On good days there was a cheerful atmosphere among the millers, and nobody minded if Barney occasionally chose to rest his weary paws by riding to the floor above on the top of a grain sack as it was winched upwards by the sturdy pulley ropes. Sometimes they jokingly added the cat's weight to pulling the enormous lever which swung the mill sails around to meet the wind. Barney would cling to the slippery ironwork for dear life,

while below him the men panted and groaned to shift the body of the rotating mill.

Despite the tough work, this was a contented and healthy existence for a dogged Capricornian. He took a pride in his valuable employment, and when he acquired a mate, a pretty Cancerian queen with whom he formed an affectionate partnership, he took care to raise their kittens in a proper appreciation of their inherited trade. The loyal generations of Barney's offspring provided the mill with skilful working cats for many a year to come.

AQUARIUS

21ST JANUARY – 19TH FEBRUARY

PLACID AQUARIANS ARE A RARE BREED, but they do exist. There are two distinct types of Aquarian, according to the ruling planet at their birth. Saturn is an ancient influence on Aquarius, producing a dependable character closely akin to Capricorn. But it is more likely that you will come across an Aquarian ruled by Uranus, the great awakener, which sends stability out of the window and endows Aquarians with a strongly made but contradictory character.

This does not make for a settled life, as the Aquarian motto could be 'change for change's sake'. The Aquarian's behaviour can be bafflingly capricious, even in the simple matter of suddenly refusing food which has been a daily favourite. This is the kind of cat which has a finely honed instinct for people who cannot abide cats: should such a person be a guest in your home, he or she will immediately become the target of a dreadful devotion conceived by your Aquarian cat, who

will stop at nothing to make its way on to the ailurophobe's lap, purring hugely, rubbing its head against your friend's hand, and padding up and down with its claw-fringed paws. This is the more disconcerting if the cat is not normally very physically affectionate, as is often the case with Aquarians, and tends to make you suspect a hint of maliciousness in the behaviour. Fortunately for your guest, Aquarians also have a low boredom threshold, and if you determinedly thwart the cat's intentions for long enough, it will decide that a change is needed and go in search of a more rewarding pastime.

Game-playing is an unavoidable aspect of life with an Aquarian, but in this context 'catch me if you can' is not a simple game of tag but a lifelong battle of wits. This does not mean that it does not indulge in physical play, such as the flying lessons off the bookshelves so beloved of felines; but an Aquarian unexpectedly hurtling through the air is in some respects easier to deal with than the cool thinker who sits on a high shelf apparently summing you up with an unblinking stare. Argu-

69

ment with an Aquarian can be the most unrewarding exercise: if the cat could speak, it would invariably expect to have the last word, but an Aquarian is also clever enough to understand the efficacy of silence as a final argument. If you have a bone to pick with your Aquarian over any aspect of its behaviour, the best tactic is simply to say your piece and then take a leaf out of its own book – give forth with a resounding silence.

There is a curious coldness to the Aquarian gaze which tells you nothing of the feelings and intentions underlying it, and since the cat will submit unconcernedly to being stroked but rarely volunteers for a cosy cuddle, you are none the wiser as to whether your Aquarian loves, hates or only tolerates you. This is in part a tactic towards self-protection, as the Aquarian can easily feel smothered by a loving companion. Time to itself and a dignified distance from expressions of affection are among the Aquarian's most valued assets, and any clumsy attempts to break down the barrier may invite an unpremeditatedly vicious response from a panicked cat. It is better to admire from afar and await the few cues which the cat will provide as to when closer companionship is appropriate. You will have no difficulty in summoning the admiration even if you are disappointed by the response, as Aquarians are often among the most beautiful of their species and are as pleasurable to view as fine paintings or delicate glass.

A similar urge to control the rules of engagement keeps the cat fairly free of neighbourhood involvement, although an interest in anything new and unexpected will take it from home often for hours at a time. Caterwauling is definitely beneath its dignity; mating relatively uninteresting; fighting for territory an unnecessary effort.

Where two or three cats are gathered together, the Aquarian is the one which merely paused as it was passing by. It will readily form acquaintanceships, though always keeping something in reserve, but will rarely feel sufficiently challenged by either the customs of the country or the aspirations of other cats to evolve deep connections with the cat community. High intelligence is an attribute of Aquarius and the cat is more interested in seeking new experience in the world, analyzing and speculating on the possibilities, than in accepting an established pattern of existence. Sociability is, however, agreeable and leaves a number of options open, and the Aquarian avoids making enemies since these can be as demanding and inhibiting as devoted friends.

Home is central to the Aquarian existence and although the cat makes its own place and moves in its own mysterious ways, it will appreciate your efforts to provide an interesting and attractive environment. Aquarians look to the future and love innovation: hi-tech surroundings will delight the Aquarian cat, which may drive you mad by its investigations, twiddling knobs and pushing buttons so that unexpectedly the blender starts whizzing in the kitchen followed by the compact disc player turning on in the living room and the electronically operated drapes passing back and forth across the window, all brought into action by an unseen hand (paw). The cat does not mind the haphazardness caused by its imperfect understanding of the point of these operations, but it should be made plain that it would be unkind to pair an Aquarian cat with a less inquiring playmate such as a Capricorn or Cancer feline, both of which would be horrified by such signs of instability in the home.

Since unpredictability is the keynote of the Aquarian character, there is no point in aiming for the perfect match in a domestic partnership. A suitable human companion for the Aquarian cat is one who will accept and even enjoy 'unnecessary' changes, whatever their sign. Despite the changeability of Aquarians, they are also surprisingly stubborn, and this can clash with the more solid fixedness of the Taurean, who also holds completely opposing values in most spheres of life.

Virgo shares an analytical tendency with Aquarius which curiously enough makes them quite unsuitable soulmates. Both need to spend their time trying to work out what makes the other tick, but neither will ever arrive at a satisfactory solution, so it's best they don't waste their time.

Libra has an excellent mental affinity with Aquarius, but Libran sensitivity can sometimes be wounded by Aquarian coolness. Aries, Gemini and Sagittarius are all signs which can both share aspects of Aquarius and let well enough alone when the circumstances seem to demand this. A Gemini may be eccentric enough in his or her own way to play against the Aquarian's capriciousness without feeling undermined; neither craves close physical contact, so will not encroach upon the other's space or feel deprived of affection. Aries appreciates Aquarian unconventionality, and enjoys the pleasures of the chase enough to enter wholeheartedly into the game-playing; nor is an Arian over-possessive, a trait guaranteed to cause claustrophobia in an Aquarian. Sagittarians are a good match in their preference for investigative activities and Aquarius can produce a kind of Sagittarian tactlessness which puts these two signs on an equal footing where emotional security is concerned.

THE BOHEMIAN CAT

*U*nconventional Aquarius likes nothing more than to be present at the birth of the future, watching a revolutionary event that shifts the pattern of life. Just such an event was occurring in the café society of Paris of the late 1860s, when a group of artists and intellectuals was engaged in heated discussions which would prove to be the beginnings of modern art. What could be more natural than that an Aquarian cat would make itself part of this vivid and innovative period, absorbing the atmosphere of excited debate as eagerly as it would devour the few scraps which might fall from the artists' plates?

Cats with their minds on more materialistic and immediate concerns could scarcely have been expected to savour the atmosphere with the same enthusiasm as the perceptive Aquarian. Most, indeed, would make it their business to be anywhere but in the vicinity of the Café Guerbois on the Thursday nights when the avant-garde assembled to thrash out their artistic preoccupations. For one thing, without prescience of the future importance of these men, a cat's main concern should have been the fact that many of the artists were virtually penniless, ordered little food and, if they did so, ate every crumb, leaving

nothing for deserving cats. One or two of the more nervous feline souls developed a notion that they might be destined to become dinner for the impoverished painter Monet if they let themselves be caught hanging around. The Aquarian cat treated such timidity with the contempt it deserved. His finer sensitivity recognized Monet as the eyes of the future, a person capable of changing the perceptions of an entire world.

Attending the meetings at the café did require a little more nimbleness than even a cat normally has to display. So vigorous were the conversations that chairs would be swung back and forth, hands and arms waved to and fro in the air, hats tumbled from heads. This added an element of physical challenge to the cat's eager appreciation of the vibrant atmosphere; more than once, absorbed in the heat of the debate, it would be swept from its perch by a burly arm flung out in enthusiasm or aggravation, causing the cat to perform a fine demonstration of its ability to twist in the air and land safely on all fours during only a very brief drop. Unfortunately, such was the self-interest of the assembled group that the cat's talents remained mainly unapplauded. Once or twice in a month it might be caressed absent-mindedly by an artist pondering his next contribution to the proceedings.

The opportunity to play more than an observer's role in these dynamic events could not fail to occur to the cat's quick brain. A regular attender at the Café Guerbois, the writer Emile Zola, was known to work at his desk with a cat at his side; perhaps it even contributed its own occult knowledge of the backstreets and alleyways of Paris to the fierce social realism of Zola's novels.

The painter Edouard Manet went one better in offering a starring role to a black cat in his painting 'Olympia'. This painting delighted the souls of all innovative Parisians by drawing the disgust of conventional critics and the art-viewing public

alike. The black cat of the 'Olympia' was singled out for attention by a myopic critic concerned to pour scorn on every aspect of the painting: 'What's to be said … for the black cat which leaves its dirty footprints on the bed?' In due course, the Aquarian cat had no doubt, the chance would arrive to leave its own mark on the culture of its time.

PISCES

ATS ARE NOT KEEN SWIMMERS, AS IS GENERALLY KNOWN, but that tiny percentage of the cat population which represents a definite exception to the rule must consist of Pisceans. This powerful Water sign can overcome a cat's natural proclivity to keep its paws dry. Even so, few cats are to be seen enthusiastically swimming laps of the garden pond, and the call of the sea may manifest itself in some curiously oblique ways to the town-bred Piscean. If you frequently encounter a startled pair of eyes peering at you over the bathtub rim at unexpected hours of the day, ten-to-one you have a Piscean on your hands.

Many cats know that the bath can be a glorious place, neatly combining a comfortable cradle with convenient toilet facilities (the cat believes this to be the function of a plughole) and a marvellous playground for catching drips from the tap or practising for a new career as a Wall of Death rider around the smooth sides of the tub.

But the Piscean, particularly, soon acquires an esoteric understanding of bathroom rituals. Its favourite trick will be to dash into the bathtub as soon as a human user has vacated, to luxuriate in the warm, damp, faintly perfumed atmosphere. If you prefer your bath without a fur lining, take your Piscean cat to live by the sea, or in the countryside close to a river or stream, and encourage it to seek its heart's desires in the natural world rather than among your plumbing arrangements.

Pisces is ruled by two planets, Jupiter and Neptune, and the influence of the former provides an easier life for those who befriend a Piscean. Jupiter makes Pisces matter-of-fact and open-hearted, a generous, expansive character.

It is perhaps more apt that Pisceans should be ruled by Neptune, the planet named for the god of the sea, but this may produce periods of oceanic turbulence rather than a calm and rhythmic existence. A Pisces can be a demanding and disruptive housemate, often without realizing it, because self-deception is a peculiarly Piscean trait. Pisceans tend to build the world as they wish it to be, whether or not this accords with external realities or the aspirations of their companions.

Seize the earliest opportunity to educate a Piscean kitten to the pleasures and problems of the real world, or it will quickly develop a fantasy land of its own from which it will never return. This kitten looks like a little angel, but really is too good to be true. It comes equipped with an internal strategy for evading guilt and retribution. Within minutes of messing on the rug, it has convinced itself that someone else did the dirty deed. It then becomes so seriously offended by the mess that it has to persuade itself that the ugly thing does not exist. In such situations you have to take immediate steps to blame the cat unequivocally and show your disapproval, as its innocence becomes more firmly established in its own mind with every passing moment.

Pisceans can be indolent and self-centred at an early age, and these tendencies should not be encouraged. A spoiled kitten may stage a fit of hysteria even if ignored only momentarily, a problem particularly acute in certain pure-bred types such as Siamese, which are proud owners of powerful complaining voices with a range that any opera singer would envy. Another trick which can become habitual is a preference for being carried, rather than walking anywhere. Pisces is the sign which influences the feet, and the cat quickly realizes that sore feet are a good excuse for travelling comfortably and under someone else's momentum — but Pisceans are also given to psychosomatic ailments, and these sensitive feet should be carefully investigated for they are probably sound and in full working order.

Such negative Piscean traits do not outweigh the fact that Pisces is one of the most emotionally open and supportive of the Zodiac signs. The Piscean cat is the one which is devotedly on hand every moment if you fall sick and have to take to your bed. It will adore the opportunity for closeness and shared comfort which attendance on the sickbed provides — and if it could cook tasty

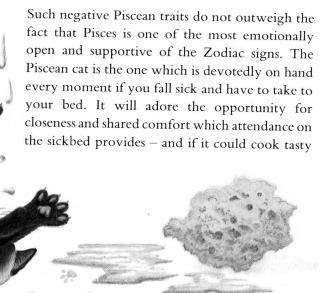

meals and kindly administer necessary medicines, undoubtedly it would. There is a changeable aspect to the Piscean personality which can produce a bewildering array of behaviour. One day the cat is moaning and wailing that it is unloved and misunderstood; the next it is all smiles and cuddles.

Pisces is a homebody by preference and will spend a lot of time around the house. A male Piscean can be a mesmeric character with an aura of energy and creativity, but this is less frequently put to use in establishing a neighbourhood presence than is the case with his Arian or Leonian counterparts. The ability to succeed in the world outside is muted by a lack of ambition and a desire for tranquillity. Female Pisceans crave comfort and home is definitely the centre of the universe as far as they are concerned. In addition, the dreamy idealism of the Piscean can be too rudely shattered by the hustle and bustle of outdoor life and the uncompromisingly direct interactions of the cat community. A feline Pisces will prefer to seek out protected places where its fantasies can be nurtured and allowed to blossom.

Indoors or out, the moods of friends and neighbours are significant to the Piscean, who is easily brought down by aggressive behaviour or a depressed atmosphere. Friendship is an important element in the life of a Pisces, but it will select its companions carefully. Against nature, the Piscean cat, especially the female, may wish to mate for life. Where deep emotions are concerned, the Piscean finds it difficult to switch allegiances, and even takes a certain masochistic pleasure in unrequited love. An unmated Pisces will happily transfer its emotional loyalties to its human provider, who can offer a continuing focus of attention.

The Pisces cat needs a combination of strength and tenderness in close partnerships, and a certain indulgence for its more whimsical or spiritual side. There is an obvious alignment between Pisces and Cancer, another Water sign with well-defined emotional needs. Both require sympathetic surroundings, and an outlet for physical expressions of sentimental attachment. Cancer will be likely to share the Piscean tendency to daydream, but the Cancerian's practical side will prevent reality from slipping away altogether.

The solidity of Taurus and dynamism of Leo offset Piscean dreaminess without harm to either party. Taurus provides passionate attention well appreciated by a Piscean, while Leo can produce a stream of thoughtful gifts, entertaining games and shared interests that prevent Pisces from making a mental escape. Virgoans are down-to-earth characters who can keep Piscean feet on the ground, but they also have an obsessive health-consciousness which appeals to the Pisces' ability to nurse and comfort others. Scorpio has a magical attraction for the spiritual side of Pisces, which may extend to telepathic capabilities. A Piscean cat should be discouraged from trying to make a home with a Gemini. The sign of the twins views the world in black-and-white, and is not at all responsive to Piscean efforts to cast a rose-tinted glow over the surroundings.

Jenny, Muse of Romance

Jenny is a pampered and fortunate creature who occupies a cat-heaven on earth, with not a cloud on her horizon; her every need is answered with generous care. This is, of course, the ideal state for a Piscean, who needs to be cushioned from the harsh realities of life. Jenny's haven came ready-made when as a tiny kitten she was invited to take up residence with a world-famous romantic novelist. This gracious lady has a talent for understanding the essence of romantic yearnings, making her a proper provider for the dreamy Piscean. Both have a firm belief in triumph over adversity and know that all the best stories have happy endings.

The environment which surrounds this pretty Piscean cat and her cherished companion is an astonishingly grand house set in beautiful parkland. In keeping with the two's preference for the soft touch, the furnishings are of silk, satin and velvet. The carpets have a pile so thick and deep that Jenny can sink into them almost up to her shoulders; the sofas are sumptuous; the beds beyond belief for their elegance and comfort. Everywhere the colours are glowing and harmonious, with gold ornaments discreetly arranged to reflect touches of brilliant light. Outdoors,

Jenny and her lady can take a companionable stroll across a well-kept parterre and into the colourful, fragrant rose garden which is the pride of the estate. On warm, sunlit days, the two of them may make their way to the delicate white summer house beside the lake to pass a shining hour in contemplation.

It should not be supposed for one moment that these two are idle in their luxury. Though they have the means to remain comfortable for life, they regard their work as a mission to lighten the load of those less fortunate than themselves. Demand for new books is as high as ever, and the lady novelist's invention seems unlikely to be exhausted as long as her faithful readers continue to look forward to fresh tales of high romance. Every day is a working day, therefore, with a quota of words to be fulfilled before the leisure hours can be enjoyed.

Jenny takes an intelligent interest in her lady's work; indeed, she is a valued assistant and commentator. The writing is done at a vast polished oak desk, on a special supply of eggshell blue paper on which the novelist writes in violet ink in her elegant script. Jenny has a special place on the desk-top from which she watches the fluid passage of the pen; she provides sympathetic support at difficult moments and an approving presence when all is going well.

The most thrilling time for Jenny is when a section of the manuscript is fully assembled to be read aloud. This is part of the novelist's pattern; she needs to hear the authentic voice of her characters before she approves the draft for preparation of a typescript, and Jenny is privileged to be the first to hear a new work unfold. The lady settles herself comfortably on a sumptuous chaise longue, Jenny on a softly padded chair. Each is equipped for these sessions with a refreshing supply of natural spring water and a little tasty nourishment to be sampled as they proceed through the taxing task.

Jenny's eyes widen as they reach the part where the heroine is separated from her loved one and cast into danger. Each time, she feels the rising anxiety as evil intervention threatens to snatch the expected happy ending from the heroine's grasp. Jenny's ears flatten, her sides heave with the emotion of the moment – and oh, the relief when the square-jawed hero in the nick of time confronts the terrible situation and restores his one true love to safety. The tension eases, the participants relax. Following the example of their fictional favourites, they take a moment to breathe in the comfort and security of their surroundings and then go to bed happy, looking forward to the dawn of another hopeful day.

ACKNOWLEDGEMENTS

We wish to thank the main contributors to this book –
Susan Robertson for providing the illustrations on pages
1, 2, 3, 4, 6, 8, 9, 11, 13, 14, 15, 16, 20, 21, 22, 26, 27, 29,
31, 32, 33, 34, 38, 39, 41, 44, 45, 47, 50, 51, 52,
56, 57, 59, 62, 63, 64, 68, 69, 71, 74, 75, 76 and 80, in
addition to the details that appear throughout the book.
John Francis for providing the illustrations on pages 19, 25,
37, 43, 49, 55, 61, 67, 73 and 79.
Russell Grant for agreeing to write the Foreword and trusting
us not to compromise his astrological philosophy.
And, finally, Judy Martin for the considerable effort she
expended in the cause of meticulous research. A long-time
(and often uncomfortably close) observer of cat-human
relationships, she may yet help to catalyse what is still a
very confused area of study.

Text by Judy Martin
Edited by Tessa Rose
Design by Alyson Kyles
Production by Garry Lewis